Refreshing Water from Ancient Wells

Refreshing Water from Ancient Wells

The Wisdom of Women Mystics

Compiled and Edited by
Mary E. Penrose, OSB

Paulist Press
New York/Mahwah, N.J.

Scripture extracts are taken from the New Revised Standard Version, Copyright © 1989, by the Division of Christian Education of the National Council of the Churches of Christ in the United States of America and reprinted by permission of the publisher.

Cover and book design by Lynn Else

Excerpts from *A Lost Tradition: Women Writers of the Early Church* reprinted by permission of Mr. Ronald Kastner. Excerpts from *Complete Works of Saint Teresa of Jesus* reprinted by permission of Sheed and Ward, an Apostolate of the Priests of the Sacred Heart, 7373 South Lovers Lane Rd., Franklin, Wisconsin, 53132. Excerpts from *Hildegard of Bingen's Book of Divine Works with Letters and Songs*, edited by Matthew Fox, published by Bear & Co., a subsidiary of Inner Traditions International, Rochester, Vermont 05767, © 1987 Bear & Company, Inc. Excerpts from *Wisdom of the Celtic Saints*, Edward C. Sellner, © 1993 by Ave Maria Press, P.O. Box 428, Notre Dame, Indiana 46556. Used with permission of the publisher. Excerpt from *A Short Breviary*, Saint John's Abbey Press, Collegeville, Minnesota, © 1975. Excerpt from *A Word in Season*, Vol. V., Augustinian Press, Villanova, Pennsylvania, © 1995. Excerpts from *Silent Voices, Sacred Lives*, Barbara Bowe, RCSJ, Kathleen Hughes, RCSJ, Sharon Karam, RCSJ, Carolyn Osiek, RCSJ, Paulist Press, Mahwah, New Jersey 07430, © 1992. Excerpts from *Medieval Women Writers*, edited by Katharina M.Wilson, University of Georgia Press, Athens, Georgia, © 1984 by the University of Georgia Press. Excerpts from *Birgitta of Sweden: Life and Selected Writings*, edited by Maguerite Tjader Harris, translated by Albert Ryle Kezel, © 1979, 1980, 1988, 1990, 1993 from the *Classics of Western Spirituality Series*, Paulist Press, Mahwah, New Jersey 07430.

Library of Congress Cataloging-in-Publication Data

Refreshing water from ancient wells : the wisdom of women mystics / compiled and edited by Mary E. Penrose.
    p. cm.
Includes bibliographical references.
ISBN 0-8091-4224-4 (alk. paper)
1. Spiritual life—Christianity. 2. Mysticism. I. Penrose, Mary, 1924-

BV4501.3.R44 2004
242—dc22

2004005241

Published by Paulist Press
997 Macarthur Boulevard
Mahwah, New Jersey 07430

www.paulistpress.com

Printed and bound in the United States of America

Table of Contents

Dedication

*With deep gratitude to Lou, Maureen, and Barb,
who have always been upbeat and affirming
confidants on my journey through life.*

Acknowledgments

I want to thank Father Lawrence Boadt, CSP, publisher of Paulist Press, for his kindness and unfailing patience in dealing with the various and sometimes complicated aspects associated with this publication. I am also grateful to his helpful and congenial staff members and to Rachel Applegate and Todd White, on the library staff of the College of St. Scholastica, Duluth, Minnesota, who gave me invaluable assistance during the project, both in the area of research and advice. My thanks, too, to Sister Maureen Truland, OSB, who located needed materials not immediately accessible to me, and to Sister Ruth Fox, OSB, who, in addition to writing the foreword, made excellent editorial suggestions and comments from time to time. Finally, I would like to thank my prioress, Sister Kathleen Hofer, OSB, and my community for their support in giving me the time and resources to work on this collection of excerpts. Special mention needs to be given to Sister Mary Odile Cahoon who came to the rescue during episodes of computer/printer problems.

Foreword

One of my favorite pictures that hung in our family home was a print of *The Gleaners* by the nineteenth-century French artist Jean-Francoise Millet. After the death of my parents, I claimed the painting and installed it in my bedroom as a memory of home. Although I have always treasured the picture, only recently have I recognized the inspiring message it continues to convey.

The painting features three peasant women in a field who are stooping to gather grain that the harvesters left behind. In the background, one can see stacks of straw and grain surrounded by several men who have already harvested the fields. The men who reaped the field ahead of these women judged the marginal grains to be unprofitable and not worth their time. However, the women found value in that which was considered insignificant, negligible, and unimportant.

In the field of the church, predominantly male harvesters have taken care to collect the biographies and writings of men through the centuries. There are libraries full of books by and about male saints and theologians. Meanwhile, the lives and writings of women have mainly been left on the margins of the church's history and teaching. They have been passed over, neglected, and forgotten on the edge of the field so that their books occupy only a small shelf in the library.

Sister Mary E. Penrose is a contemporary gleaner in the field of the church. She has gathered a wealth of writings by and about women from early Christian centuries to the present. Using the skills of a dedicated gleaner, she hunted, searched, and scrounged through countless printed resources.

She then gathered samples of her findings into this valuable little book to bring us some unexpected riches.

Some of the women's names included in this collection will be familiar to most readers, such as Catherine of Siena and Teresa of Avila. Other names such as Proba, Syncletica, and Ameliana will probably be unfamiliar. Readers will be introduced to some fresh insights and reflections from women of all ages and cultures. For example, ponder this little gem from a ninth-century French woman known as Dhouda:

> To be sure, if the heavens and the earth were spread through the air like a parchment, and if all various gulfs of the sea were transformed into ink, and if all the inhabitants of the earth born into this world from the beginning of humankind up to now were scribes— which is impossible—they would not be able to comprehend [in writing] the greatness, the breadth, the height, the sublimity, the profundity of the Almighty.

While the passages are relatively short, my hope is that the readers will enjoy the samples so much that they will want to search out the sources and do their own gleaning to find the rest of the story. After each selected passage, Penrose has thoughtfully provided readers with additional selections from scripture or other sources to further develop the theme. For those persons responsible for finding readings for special feasts and occasions, she has again provided suggestions when the passage might be useful. The book can be a resource for those who plan prayer services and liturgies. It can also profitably be used for an individual's personal daily reflection. Probably women will find this collection most enriching, but men will also discover in the gleanings some nourishing words for their journey.

Enjoy the harvest collected by Sister Mary E. Penrose, the gleaner. And be aware that there are more fields to be cleaned.

Ruth M. Fox, OSB

Sister Ruth Fox, OSB, has been a member of Sacred Heart Monastery, Richardton, North Dakota, for nearly fifty years. She has served as prioress of her community, president of the Federation of St. Gertrude, and president of the American Benedictine Academy. Currently, she is director of the ecumenical Spirituality Center at her monastery, and also finds time to write and speak in the area of feminine and monastic spirituality.

Introduction

St. Benedict, modestly claiming that he wrote a "little rule for beginners" (*Rule of Benedict*, chapter 73.8), gives primacy of place to scripture as a guide for human life. However, he adds, "What book of the holy catholic Fathers does not resoundingly summon us along the true way to reach the Creator?" (73.4). Today, fortunately, modern scholarship allows us to add to these the writings of the Mothers.

The words of wisdom found here from our early women ancestors in the faith can be used as alternative readings for the Liturgical Hours, for paraliturgies, other prayer services, or simply for *lectio* or private meditation. The readings are not limited to the exclusive use of those in religious life, though frequently religious do express a desire for more variety in the readings assigned for use at community prayer. These readings may fill that gap. After experimenting with some of them at the Hours, I have been both rewarded and amused to hear such comments as, "Where did you find that reading?" "I never heard that before!" "Did she really say that?" and so on.

Another frequently expressed wish is that readings used for liturgy would be shorter, more adapted to the attention span of ordinary listeners. In view of this, these readings are either short excerpts taken from longer readings or longer readings that have been edited to make them shorter and more readable. Inclusive language has been used whenever possible, and archaic words have been modified to make them more understandable.

The suggested readings (from scripture or other sources) correspond in tone and topic with the preceding liturgical reading. They also are less lengthy. Since they are paired, both sets of readings can be used on the same day, or they can be used separately according to the discretion of those using them. Readers might want to add other readings (as well as occasions) if they find them more suitable. Passages from the gospel are not included because it is assumed these readings, if used publicly, will be utilized at times other than the eucharistic celebration. Of course, judiciously chosen, they can also support the gospel proclaimed at the Eucharist.

All these comments are suggestions only. They are made in the spirit of St. Benedict who said, in regard to the arrangement of the Divine Office, "Above all else we urge that if anyone finds this distribution of the psalms unsatisfactory, they should arrange whatever they judge better..." (*Rule of Benedict*, chapter 18.22). Whatever way readers decide to quench their thirst at these ancient wells will give this author great pleasure.

Mary E. Penrose, OSB

Reflections

Aemiliana Löhr

(Themes—Wisdom, Mary)

If God wanted to reveal his maternal aspect to us—whether we call it Wisdom, or Love, or whatever name we give it—in a womanly maternal form; if he wanted to grant us salvation from the womb of Mary and from the womb of the Church, then God has done so by setting before us a powerful and compelling image, a model for our whole material as well as spiritual life. It is to be a bridal and maternal life that blossoms and bears fruit out of the fullness of God's being and grace, and moreover for all of us, man as well as woman, since man too is a created being and therefore a bride before God.[1]

SUGGESTED READINGS	SUGGESTED OCCASIONS
Hos 2:16–20	Feasts of Mary
Rev 21:1–6	Pentecost
Acts 2:14–21	Feasts of virgins

Anahid

(Themes—Suffering, Spirituality)

While Anahid was in prison…she spent the night praising God until morning.…When morning came, the nobles assembled and sent for the holy woman. Since she could not walk because of the fetters, they had to carry her into their presence. Once she had been set down in front of them, they urged her to abandon the doctrines she clung to. Some of them used threats, others cajoled her, while one of them, a close relative of hers, went up to her and said, "My daughter Anahid, what is the matter with you, what has happened to you that you act differently from everyone else? If they have eliminated your father...and he has met a bad end, what demon has got hold of you? ...at least say, 'I am not a Christian,' and then I can save you and carry you off to somewhere where there are Christians, and you can live there in Christianity all the rest of your life."

The wise woman replied, "You silly and senseless man, how can I deny God in whom we live and move and have our being (Acts 17:28)? Where can I go to where God is not there; what place is there that is not filled with God and God is not there? Furthermore, our Lord Christ said that 'those who deny me before others, I will deny before my Father in heaven' (Matt 10:33). As it is, I have already renounced your gods—which are not gods—and I continue to do so; and I have confessed Him and will continue to confess Him right up to death."[2]

SUGGESTED READINGS   SUGGESTED OCCASIONS
Acts 12:1–8   Martyrs
2 Tim 2:8–13   Time of trial

Angela Merici

(Theme—Service)

Dear mothers and sisters in Christ Jesus: Strive above all, with God's help, to be guided solely by love of God and zeal for souls in doing your work. Only if your work is rooted and grounded in this twofold love will your concern and guidance bear good fruit for salvation.

I urge you to look to the needs of each child and to have engraved in your hearts not only their names but their home environment and differing personalities as well. This will be no problem if you have a lively love for them. Women who are mothers in the flesh may have a thousand children, yet bear each in their hearts and never forget a single one of them. That is how love works. Show sweetness to all. Above all, do not force your commands on others. God has given each person freedom and forces no one, but only indicates, calls and persuades. Even when severer measures are needed, charity and zeal must show how they are to be applied.[3]

SUGGESTED READINGS	SUGGESTED OCCASIONS
Rom 12:9–18	New academic year
Col 3:12–17	Educational meetings
	Angela's feast—January 27

Birgitta of Sweden

(Themes—Spirituality, Stewardship)

The Mother speaks: "Daughter, you must have five inward things and five outward. First outwardly: a mouth clean of all detraction, ears closed to idle talk, modest eyes, hands busy with good works, and withdrawal from the world's way of life. Inwardly, you must have five things: namely, fervent love for God, a wise longing for God, the distribution of your temporal goods with a just and right intention and in a rational way, humble flight from the world, and a long-suffering and patient expectation of my promises."[4]

SUGGESTED READINGS	SUGGESTED OCCASIONS
Acts 4:32–37	Days of prayer
Prov 10:6–14	Ordinary time
Eph 5:1–11	Birgitta's feast—July 23

Birgitta of Sweden

(Themes—Suffering, Trials)

As to why adverse things befall the just, I answer: My justice is that the just should obtain what they seek. But no one is just who does not desire to suffer adverse things for the sake of obedience and the perfection of justice and who does not do good to their neighbor. My friends consider what I their God and Redeemer have done for them and what I have promised. Also, they are attentive to wickedness in the world. As a precaution, they more gladly seek—for my honor, for their own salvation, and for the avoidance of sin—the adverse things of the world rather than its prosperity. Therefore I permit tribulations to befall them. If some of them suffer with too little patience, I do not permit this to happen without a reason; and I stand by them in their trouble. When children in childhood are rebuked by their mother, they do not know enough to thank her because they cannot weigh the cause for which they are being reproved. But when they have reached the age of discretion, they thank their mother because through her instruction they have been drawn away from wrongdoing and have become accustomed to discipline and good behavior.

I treat my elect in a similar way. When they entrust their will to me and love me above all things, they have tribulations for a time. They may not fully understand my benefactions at present; nevertheless I am doing what is best for them in the future....However, not all the wicked are given what they desire—in order that they may know that it lies within my power to give gifts to whomever I will. For I can grant good things even to the ungrateful though they do not deserve them.[5]

SUGGESTED READINGS	SUGGESTED OCCASIONS
Job 34:2–17	Lent
Rom 5:1–11	Birgitta's feast—July 23
1 Pet 5:1–11	Time of trial

Birgitta of Sweden

(Themes—Stewardship, Simplicity)

As to why you must not take pride in riches, I answer: the world's riches are yours only for your necessary nourishment and clothing. The world was made in order that you—having sustenance for your body—might return, by means of labor and humility, to me, your God, whom you disobediently despised and for whom, in your pride, you had no care. Moreover, if you say that temporal goods are yours, I tell you for certain that you, as it were, violently usurp for yourself all those things which you have beyond your necessities. For all temporal goods ought to be common and, out of charity, equal for those in need. But you superfluously usurp for yourself things that should be given to others out of compassion.

Still, it is feasible that many people have much more than others; they own it reasonably and they distribute it with discretion. Therefore, for fear you be reproved more gravely at the judgment because you have received greater things than others, you are advised not to put yourself above others by boasting and by hoarding.[6]

SUGGESTED READINGS	SUGGESTED OCCASIONS
Isa 23:13–18	Birgitta's feast—July 23
Jas 5:1–8	Social justice days
Rule of Benedict,	Undertaking a new task
Prologue 1–7	

Birgitta of Sweden

(Themes—Leisure, Spirituality)

As to why it is not always daylight, I will answer you by means of an example. Under every vehicle, e.g., a cart, there are wheels so that the burden placed upon it may be more easily moved; and the back wheels follow those in front. A similarity exists in spiritual matters. For the world is a great burden, weighing us down with worries and troubles. And no wonder, for when we disdain the place of rest, it is right that we experience a place of work. Therefore, in order that the burden of this world may be more easily borne, mercifully there comes a change and alternation of times—namely: day and night, summer and winter—for the sake of our exercise and our rest....

So it is with us. Even though, in the strength of our immortal soul, we could continue forever in contemplation and labor, nevertheless the strength of our weak bodies would fail. For this reason, light has been made so that we, who have a common bond with higher and lower beings, may be able to subsist by laboring in the day, while remembering the sweetness of the everlasting light that we lost. Night has been made that we may rest our body with the hope of coming to that place where there is neither night nor labor, but rather, everlasting day and eternal glory.[7]

SUGGESTED READINGS   SUGGESTED OCCASIONS

SUGGESTED READINGS	SUGGESTED OCCASIONS
Isa 45:2–8	Labor Day
1 John 1:3–10	Birgitta's feast—July 23
	Winter solstice

Birgitta of Sweden

(Themes—Spirituality, Pentecost)

As to why I [Jesus] willed to be baptized, I answer: everyone who wills to establish or begin a new way must—as the establisher of that way—walk on it ahead of others. For the ancient People, a physical way, namely, circumcision, was given as a sign of obedience and future purgation. In faithful persons who kept the law, it fashioned something of the future grace and promise before the coming of that promised Truth itself—namely, myself, the Son of God. Because the law was only, as it were, a shadow, it had been determined in eternity that with the coming of Truth, the ancient way, lacking its effectiveness, would disappear. Therefore, that the Truth might appear, the shadow yielded, and an easier way to heaven was manifested.

I, God and human, born without sin, willed to be baptized out of humility and as an example to others so that heaven might be opened to those who believe. As a sign of this, when I was baptized, the heavens were opened; the Father's voice was heard; the Holy Spirit appeared in the form of a dove; and I, God's Son, was manifested as truly human that all the faithful might know and believe that the Father opens heaven for the faithful who have been baptized....And so, when I, Truth itself, came into the world, then, at once, the shadow vanished, the shell of the law was broken and the kernel appeared. Circumcision gave way and in me baptism was confirmed, through which heaven is opened for the young and the old, and the children of wrath become children of grace and of life everlasting.[8]

SUGGESTED READINGS	SUGGESTED OCCASIONS
Acts 8:9–19	Baptism of Jesus
Acts 11:1–18	Pentecost season
Rom 3:1–9, 19–20	Birgitta's feast—July 23

Birgitta of Sweden

(Themes—Suffering, Penance)

As to why I did not show the power of my Godhead and the truth of my divinity to all when, on the cross, I said: "It is consummated," I answer: all that was written about me had to be fulfilled. Therefore, I fulfilled all those things even to the last point. But, because many things had been foretold about my resurrection and ascension, it was necessary that these words too should have their effect. If the power of my Godhead had been shown at my death, who would have dared to take me down from the cross and bury me? Actually, it would have been a very small matter for me to come down from the cross and scatter my crucifiers. But how, then, would prophecy have been fulfilled; and where, then, would the virtue of my patience be?

If I had come down from the cross, would all have really believed? Would they not have said that I had used an evil skill? For if they were indignant because I raised the dead and healed the sick, they would have said even worse things if I had come down from the cross. Therefore, that captives might be loosed, I—the free—was captured; and that the guilty might be saved, I—the guiltless—stayed fast upon the cross. And through my steadfastness, I steadied all that was unstable and strengthened the weak.[9]

SUGGESTED READINGS	SUGGESTED OCCASIONS
Heb 7:18–28	Feast of Holy Cross
Heb 4:8–16	Lent
Heb 5:1–10	Times of trial

Birgitta of Sweden

(Themes—Temptation, Trials)

It is written that Jacob worked as a servant for Rachel's sake and that the days seemed few to him because of his great love; for the greatness of his love lightened his labors. But just when Jacob believed that he had attained his desire, he was outwitted; nevertheless, he did not cease from his labor because love does not debate about difficulty until it reaches what it desires. So it is in spiritual matters. To obtain the things of heaven, many labor powerfully in prayers and pious works, but when they think that they have attained the repose of contemplation, they become involved in temptations. Their tribulations increase; and just when they are considering themselves almost perfect, they find that they are totally imperfect. No wonder, for it is temptations that probe and purge and perfect us.

For some, temptations increase in the beginning of their conversion to the spiritual life. Such persons become more perfectly strengthened in the end. Others are more gravely tempted in the middle of their lives and at the end. These must observe themselves carefully, never presuming anything about themselves, laboring all the more bravely. As Laban said: "It is the custom to take the elder sister first." It was as if he were to say: "First practice labor, and afterward you will have the repose you desire." Therefore, daughter, you are not to marvel if even in old age temptations increase. For as long as life is permitted, temptation too is possible. And temptation is an opportunity for perfection so that we do not become presumptuous.[10]

SUGGESTED READINGS   **SUGGESTED OCCASIONS**

Gen 29:14b–28   Renewal days

Jas 1:12–19   Lent

                                                  Ordinary time

Birgitta of Sweden

(Themes—Wisdom, Holiness)

As to why some have greater intelligence I answer: The abundance of one's wisdom does not profit the soul toward eternal salvation unless the soul also shines with a good life. On the contrary, it is more useful to have less knowledge and a better life. Each person has been given a measure of knowledge by means of which they can obtain heaven if they live devoutly. However, intelligence varies in many according to their natural and spiritual dispositions....Many times nature suffers a defect when one strives against nature and one sins. Therefore, it is not without cause that in some, logic is great but useless, as in those who have knowledge but not life. In others, there is less knowledge but better practice. In some, of course, knowledge and life are in agreement....

In youth, Peter the apostle was forgetful and John was no trained expert; but they grasped true wisdom in their old age because they searched for wisdom's beginning. When young, Solomon was docile and Aristotle was subtle; but they did not grasp the beginning of wisdom because they neither glorified the Giver of knowledge as they ought, nor imitated the things that they knew and taught. Balaam, too, had knowledge but did not follow it; therefore the she-ass rebuked his folly. Daniel when young, judged his elders. Erudition, without a good life, does not please me; therefore, it is necessary that those who abuse knowledge be corrected. For I, the God and Lord of all, give knowledge to humankind; and I correct both the wise and the foolish.[11]

SUGGESTED READINGS	SUGGESTED OCCASIONS
1 Kgs 10:1–10	Pentecost season
Num 22:22–34	Ordinary time
Prov 3:13–24	Days of discernment

Birgitta of Sweden

(Themes—Prayer, Liturgy)

As to why my friends, petitioning me in their prayers, are not always heard by me, I answer: I am like a mother who sees her child making a request contrary to their welfare. I put off listening to the petition while, at the same time, checking their tears with some indignation. Such indignation is not anger but great mercy. I do not always hear my friends because I see—better than they do—the things that are more useful for their welfare.

Did not Paul and others pray with energy and yet were not heard? Why? Because in the midst of their abundant virtues, my friends had certain weaknesses needing to be purged. Therefore they are not heard in order that they may be all that more humble and fervent toward me, the more lovingly they are defended by me and preserved unscathed in temptations to sin.

It is therefore a sign of great love that the prayers of my friends are not always heard—for the sake of their greater merit and for the proving of their constancy. Just as the devil tries, if possible, to spoil the life of the just through some sin or through a contemptible death in order that the constancy of the faithful will grow tepid, so too I permit, not without cause, the testing of the just in order that their stability may be known to others and that they themselves may be more sublimely crowned.[12]

SUGGESTED READINGS	SUGGESTED OCCASIONS
Jas 5:13–20	Prayer days
Jas 1:2–7, 12–15	Lent
	Birgitta's feast—July 23

Birgitta of Sweden

(Themes—Mary, Advent)

That vessel of which I spoke to you was Mary…the mother of Christ. She was indeed a vessel closed and not closed: closed to the devil but not to God. For just as a torrent of water—wishing to enter a vessel opposed to it and not being able—seeks other ways in and out, so the devil's torrent of vices wished to approach Mary's heart by means of numerous inventions. But it was not possible to incline her soul toward even the slightest sin because it had been closed against all temptations. For the torrent of my Spirit had flowed into her heart and filled her with special grace. Second, Mary, the mother of my Son, was a vessel small and not small: small and modest in her lowliness; great and not small in love for my Godhead. Third, Mary was a vessel empty and not empty: empty of all self-indulgence and sin; not empty but full of heavenly sweetness and all goodness.

Fourth, Mary was a vessel luminous and not luminous: luminous because every beautiful soul is created by me; but Mary's soul so grew toward the full perfection of light that my Son fixed himself in her soul, at whose beauty heaven and earth rejoiced. However, this vessel was not luminous in the sight of humankind because she scorned the world's honors and wealth. Fifth, Mary was a vessel clean and not clean: truly clean because she was all beautiful and because there was not found in her even enough uncleanness in which to fix the point of a needle; not clean because she came forth from Adam's root and was born of sinners, although she herself was conceived without sin in order that, of her, my Son might be born without sin.[13]

SUGGESTED READINGS	SUGGESTED OCCASIONS
Rom 6:10–23	Feasts of Mary
Rom 7:4–15	Advent

Brigitta of Sweden

(Themes—Renewal, Discernment)

On the feast of Saint Francis, in his church in Trastevere in Rome, Saint Francis appeared to the bride of Christ [i.e., Brigitta] and said to her, "Come into my chamber to eat and to drink with me." When she heard this, she at once prepared for a journey in order to visit him in Assisi. After she had stayed there five days, she decided to return to Rome and entered the church to recommend herself and her loved ones to Saint Francis. He then appeared to her and said: "Welcome! For I invited you into my chamber to eat and to drink with me. Know, however, that this building is not the chamber that I mentioned to you. No, my chamber is true obedience, which I held so strongly that I never endured being without an instructor. For I continually had with me a priest whose every instruction I humbly obeyed, and this was my chamber. Therefore, do likewise for this is pleasing to God."[14]

SUGGESTED READINGS	SUGGESTED OCCASIONS
Eccl 1:11	Feast of St. Francis
1 Pet 1:13–21	Renewal days
Rom 6:14–21	
Rule of Benedict,	
chapter 5.1–13	

Brigitta of Sweden

(Themes—Moderation, Penance)

By the gates of the house I mean, in fact, all the body's needs, which indeed the body cannot refuse: namely, eating, drinking, sleep, wakefulness, and even occasional distresses and joys. The guardian, reason, must stand by these gates—that is, the body's needs—with concern and, with holy fear, must resist enemies wisely and persistently lest they enter the soul. Just as in taking food and drink one must beware for fear the enemy enter through overindulgence, which makes the soul slothful in serving God, so too one must beware lest the foe gain entrance through excessive abstinence, which makes the body weak in doing all things. Let the guardian, reason, also take note for fear that, either when alone with your household or when guests arrive, there be an uninterrupted succession of too many courses at meals for the sake of worldly honor and the favorable opinion of others. Rather, out of divine charity, treat each one well while excluding multiplicity of foods and also extravagant delicacies.

Next the guardian, reason, must with vigilance and attention consider the fact that, just as food and drink must be moderated, so too must sleep be moderated that the body may be nimble and in better order. In this way every waking moment may accomplish the honor of God by being usefully spent on the divine offices and on honest labors, with the heaviness of sleep far removed.[15]

SUGGESTED READINGS	SUGGESTED OCCASIONS
1 Cor 8:6–13	Advent
1 Cor 10:1–13	Lent
1 Tim 3:1–13	Ordinary time

Birgitta of Sweden

(Themes—Penance, Mary)

Honor be to you, my Lady, O Virgin Mary. In sorrow, you gazed at your Son as he spoke to you from the cross; and with your blessed ears, you sadly heard him, in the agony of death, crying to the Father and commending his own soul into his hands.

Praise be to you, my Lady, O Virgin Mary. With bitter sorrow, you saw your Son hanging on the cross: from the top of his head to the soles of his feet, all black and blue and marked with the red of his own blood, and so cruelly dead. You also gazed at the bitter sight of the holes in his feet, in his hands, and even in his glorious side. You gazed at his skin, all lacerated without any mercy.

Blessed may you be, my Lady, O Virgin Mary. With tears in your eyes, you saw your Son taken down, wrapped in cloths, buried in a monument, and there guarded by soldiers.

Blessed may you be, my Lady, O Virgin Mary. To the grave intensification of your heart's deep sorrow, you parted from the sepulcher of your Son and, full of grief, were brought by his friends to the house of John. But there, at once, you felt a relief of your great sorrow because you most surely knew that your Son would quickly rise.[16]

SUGGESTED READINGS	SUGGESTED OCCASIONS
Jer 31:15–17	Our Lady of Sorrows
Prov 4:5–13	Lent

Birgitta of Sweden

(Themes—Penance, Mary)

O my Lady, most fertile and most virginal Virgin Mary, blessed be your most blessed womb above all fruitfully sprouting fields. Just as the seed that has fallen upon good ground brings forth for its owner fruit a hundredfold, even so your womb, a virgin-womb and yet most fertile, brought forth for God blessed fruit, more than a thousandfold.

Just as the lord of a field glories in its fertile abundance of fruit and just as the little birds and the animals feed in it with delight, even so did the blessed and fertile fruit of the little field of your womb cause high honor for God in heaven, rejoicing for the angels and for humans on earth, a lavish flow of sustenance and life.

And you, my Lord, my King, and my God, to you be perpetual honor, perennial praise, blessing and glory, and infinite thanksgiving. For you created this Virgin so worthy and so honest; and you chose her for yourself as your Mother for the sake of all who in any way have been consoled in heaven and on earth.[17]

SUGGESTED READINGS	SUGGESTED OCCASIONS
1 Sam 2:1–10	Advent
Rom 4:18–24	Feasts of Mary
	Birgitta's feast—July 23

Blandina

(Themes—Suffering, Commitment)

The blessed martyrs underwent torments beyond all description....All of us were in terror; and Blandina's earthly mistress, who was herself among the martyrs in the conflict, was in agony lest because of her bodily weakness she would not be able to make a bold confession of her faith. Yet Blandina was filled with such power that even those who were taking turns to torture her in every way from dawn to dusk were weary and exhausted. They themselves admitted that they were beaten, that there was nothing further they could do to her, and they were surprised that she was still breathing, for her entire body was broken and torn. They testified that even one kind of torture was enough to release her soul, let alone the many they applied with such intensity. Instead, this blessed woman like a noble athlete, got renewed strength with her confession of faith; her admission, "I am a Christian; we do nothing to be ashamed of" brought her refreshment, rest and insensibility to her present pain.[18]

SUGGESTED READINGS	SUGGESTED OCCASIONS
Job 36:5–15	Martyrs' feasts
Isa 53:3–7	Witness/commitment
	Blandina's feast—June 2

Blandina

(Themes—Suffering, Perseverance)

Blandina was hung on a post and exposed as bait for the wild animals that were let loose on her. She seemed to hang there in the form of a cross, and by her fervent prayer she aroused intense enthusiasm in those who were undergoing their ordeal, for in their torment with their physical eyes they saw in the person of their sister Him who was crucified for them that He might convince all who believe in Him that all who suffer for Christ's glory will have eternal fellowship in the living God.

But none of the animals had touched her, and so she was taken for another ordeal; and thus for her victory in further contests she would make irreversible the condemnation of the crooked serpent, and tiny, weak, and insignificant as she was, she would give inspiration to her brothers, for she had put on Christ, that mighty and invincible athlete, and had overcome the Adversary in many contests, and through her conflict had won the crown of immortality.[19]

Brigit of Kildare

(Themes—Wisdom, Friendship)

The following is a tale about St. Brigit who governed both men and women in her double monastery at Kildare:

A young cleric of the community of Ferns, a foster-son of Brigit's, used to come to her with wishes. He was often with her in the refectory to partake of food. One time, after coming to communion, she struck a bell. "Well, young cleric there," said Brigit, "do you have a soul friend?"

"I have," replied the young man.

"Let us sing his requiem," said Brigit, "for he has died. I saw when you had eaten half your portion of food that that portion was put in the trunk of your body, but that you were without any head. For your soul friend has died, and anyone without a soul friend is like a body without a head. Eat no more until you get a soul friend."[20]

Catherine of Genoa

(Themes—Prayer, Spirituality)

A ray of God's love wounded Catherine's heart, making her soul experience a flaming love arising from the divine fount. At that instant, she was outside of herself, beyond intellect, tongue, or feeling. Fixed in that pure and divine love, from then on she never ceased to dwell on it.

She was also made to understand the extent of her ingratitude and mirrored herself in her sins; she was overcome with such despair and self-loathing that she was tempted to publicly confess her sins. She cried out, "O Lord, no more world, no more sins!"

She did not view sins principally as sins but as offenses against the goodness of God, God's strong love. It was the consciousness of that that made her turn against herself, and do her utmost to translate that love into deeds.[21]

<table>
<tr><td>**SUGGESTED READINGS**</td><td>**SUGGESTED OCCASIONS**</td></tr>
<tr><td>Jas 2:14–23</td><td>Renewal days</td></tr>
<tr><td>1 John 3:16–23</td><td>Ordinary time</td></tr>
<tr><td></td><td>Catherine's feast—</td></tr>
<tr><td></td><td>September 14</td></tr>
</table>

Catherine of Genoa

(said twelve days before she died)

(Themes—Trials, Suffering)

> Let every suffering and pain be welcome that comes
>   from God's will,
> for you have illuminated me, O Lord,

for the last thirty-six years or so.
For your sake I have always sought to suffer,
   within as well as without.
And this desire has never let me suffer greatly.
On the contrary, all those things that I have undergone
   that seemed intense suffering
were, because of your will, sweet and consoling.
Now that I am at the end
and seem to be in such pain from head to toe
that it would seem that the body could not endure it
and would be about to die and be quite annihilated,
I see that you who rule over all things with your will
   do not want me to die as yet.
So that in the midst of the pain my body endures,
without comfort of any kind,
I still cannot say that I am suffering.
You make all things bearable,
and my joy is such that it cannot be imagined or
   expressed.[22]

SUGGESTED READINGS	SUGGESTED OCCASIONS
2 Cor 4:7–14	Times of trial
Rom 8:18–23	Lent
	Catherine's feast—
	September 14

Catherine of Genoa

(Themes—Love, Prayer)

Then Catherine was made to experience a spark of that Pure Love with which God had created it. That experience imparted such fire to her heart that all woes left her and she burned with a fire of that love which God had her experience. She so passionately answered that love that her heart was brimming over, utterly absorbed in that exchange, and the Soul came close to leaving the body, leaving the earth and transforming itself into God. Whereupon her humanity said:

> You are endangering me to excess.
> I feel the roots that attach me to life cut,
>   and find myself quite abandoned.
> All you do is concentrate on heaven and forget me.
> It seems to me that you seek to undo me with fiery arrows
> that pierce me to the quick.
> You make me cry out in pain,
> and would have me go scurrying about madly on all
>   fours.[23]

SUGGESTED READINGS	SUGGESTED OCCASIONS
Jer 20:7–13	Prayer days
Job 19:13–21	Catherine's feast—
	September 14
	Ordinary time

Catherine of Siena

(Themes—Love, Suffering)

[Eternal Truth speaking to Catherine] I have shown you, dearest daughter, that in this life guilt is not atoned for by any suffering simply as suffering, but rather by suffering borne with desire, love and contrition of heart. The value is not in the suffering but in the soul's desire. Likewise, neither desire nor any other virtue has value or life except through my only-begotten Son, Christ crucified, since the soul has drawn love from him and in virtue follows his footsteps. In this way and in no other is suffering of value. It satisfies for sin, then, with gentle unitive love born from the sweet knowledge of my goodness and from the bitterness and contrition the heart finds in the knowledge of itself and its own sins. Such knowledge gives birth to hatred and contempt for sin and for the soul's selfish sensuality....So you see, said gentle Truth, those who have heartfelt contrition, love for true patience, and that true humility which considers oneself worthy of punishment and unworthy of reward suffer with patience and so make atonement.[24]

SUGGESTED READINGS	SUGGESTED OCCASIONS
1 Pet 3:13–17	Lent
1 Pet 5:5–11	Communal penance
	Catherine's feast—
	April 29

Catherine of Siena

(Themes—Spirituality, Discernment)

If penance becomes the foundation [of virtue], it becomes a hindrance to perfection. Being done without the discerning light of the knowledge of oneself and of my goodness, it would fall short of my truth. It would be undiscerning, not loving what I most love and not hating what I most hate. For discernment is nothing else but the true knowledge a soul ought to have of herself and of me, and through this knowledge she finds her roots. It is joined to charity like an engrafted shoot.

Charity...has many offshoots, like a tree with many branches. But what gives life to both the tree and its branches is its root, so long as that root is planted in the soil of humility. For humility is the governess and wet nurse of the charity into which this branch of discernment is engrafted. Now the source of humility, as I have already told you, is the soul's true knowledge of herself and my goodness.[25]

SUGGESTED READINGS	SUGGESTED OCCASIONS
Prov 2:1–11	Communal penance
Wis 6:12–20	Times of discernment
	Ordinary time

Catherine of Siena

(Themes—Humility, Discernment)

Without humility, as I have said, the soul would be without discernment. For lack of discernment is set in pride, just as discernment is set in humility. A soul without discernment would, like a thief, rob me of my honor and bestow it on herself for her own glory. And what was her own doing she would blame on me, grumbling and complaining about my mysterious ways with her and with the rest of my creatures, constantly finding cause for scandal in me and in her neighbors. Not so those who have the virtue of discernment. These give what is due to me and to themselves. And then they give their neighbors what is due them: first of all, loving charity and constant humble prayer—your mutual debt—and the debt of teaching, and the example of a holy and honorable life, and the counsel and help they need for their salvation.[26]

SUGGESTED READINGS	SUGGESTED OCCASIONS
Rom 13:7–11	Discernment days
Eph 4:7–13	Peace and justice days
	Catherine's feast—
	April 29

Catherine of Siena

(Themes—Suffering, Spirituality)

Do you know what course I follow, once my servants have completely given themselves to the teaching of the gentle, loving Word? I prune them so that they will bear much fruit—cultivated fruit, not wild. Just as the gardener prunes the branch that is joined to the vine so that it will yield more and better wine, but cuts off and throws into the fire the branch that is barren, so do I the true gardener act. When my servants remain united to me I prune them with great suffering so that they will bear more and better fruit, and virtue will be proved in them....

These are the true workers. They till their souls well, uprooting every selfish love, cultivating the soil of their love in me. They feed and tend the growth of the seed of grace that they received in holy baptism. And as they till their own vineyards, so they till their neighbors as well, for they cannot do the one without the other. You already know that every evil as well as every good is done by means of your neighbors.[27]

SUGGESTED READINGS	SUGGESTED OCCASIONS
Isa 5:1–7a	Lent
Jer 31:7–12	Spring season
	Ordinary time

Catherine of Siena

(Themes—Love, Suffering)

Though this bridge has been raised so high, it still is joined to the earth....When my Son was lifted up on the wood of the most holy cross He did not cut off His divinity from the lowly earth of Your humanity. So though He was raised so high He was not raised off the earth. In fact, His divinity is kneaded into the clay of your humanity like one bread. Nor could anyone walk on that bridge until my Son was raised up. This is why He said, "If I am lifted up high I will draw everything to Myself."

When my goodness saw that you could be drawn in no other way, I sent Him to be lifted onto the wood of the cross. I made of that cross an anvil where this child of humankind could be hammered into an instrument to release humankind from death and restore it to the life of grace. In this way He drew everything to Himself: for He proved His unspeakable love, and the human heart is always drawn by love. He could not have shown you greater love than by giving His life for you. You can hardly resist being drawn by love, then, unless you foolishly refuse to be drawn.[28]

SUGGESTED READINGS	SUGGESTED OCCASIONS
Num 21:4–9	Feast of Holy Cross
Col 2:9–15	Lent

Catherine of Siena

(Themes—Mercy, Suffering)

[Catherine said...] You temper your justice with mercy. In mercy You cleansed us in the blood; in mercy You kept company with your creatures. O mad lover! It was not enough for You to take on our humanity: You had to die as well! Nor was death enough: You descended to the depths to summon our holy ancestors and fulfill your truth and mercy in them. Your goodness promises good to those who serve You in truth, so You went to call these servants of yours from their suffering to reward them for their labors!

I see your mercy pressing You to give us even more when You leave yourself with us as food to strengthen our weakness, so that we forgetful fools should be forever reminded of your goodness. Every day You give us this food, showing us yourself in the sacrament of the altar within the mystic body of holy Church. And what has done this? Your mercy.[29]

SUGGESTED READINGS	SUGGESTED OCCASIONS
Rom 11:25–32	Lent
1 Tim 1:12–17	Ordinary time

Catherine of Siena

(Themes—Love, Friendship)

The soul cannot live without love. She always wants to love something because love is the stuff she is made of, and through love I created her. This is why I said that it is affection that moves the understanding saying, as it were, "I want to love because the food I feed on is love." And the understanding, feeling itself awakened by affection, gets up, as it were, and says, "If you want to love, I will give you something good that you can love. And at once it is aroused by the consideration of the soul's dignity and the indignity into which she has fallen through her own fault. In the dignity of her existence she tastes the immeasurable goodness and uncreated love with which I created her. And in the sight of her own wretchedness she discovers and tastes my mercy, for in mercy I have lent her time and drawn her out of darkness."[30]

SUGGESTED READINGS	SUGGESTED OCCASIONS
Isa 42:1–7	Lent
Eph 5:8–17	Ordinary time
	Catherine's feast—
	April 29

Catherine of Siena

(Themes—Love, Friendship)

[God said…] I ask you to love me with the same love with which I love you. But for me you cannot do this, for I loved you without being loved. Whatever love you have for me you owe me, so you love me not gratuitously but out of duty, while I love you not out of duty but gratuitously. So you cannot give me the kind of love I ask of you. This is why I have put you among your neighbors: so that you can do for them what you cannot do for me—that is, love them without any concern for thanks and without looking for any profit for yourself. And whatever you do for them I will consider done for me. My Truth demonstrated this when Paul was persecuting me and he said, "Saul, Saul, why are you persecuting me?"

Your love should be sincere: You should love your neighbors with the same love with which you love me. Do you know how you can tell when your spiritual love is not perfect? If you are distressed when it seems that those you love are not returning your love or not loving you as much as you think you love them. Or if you are distressed when it seems to you that you are being deprived of their company or comfort, or that they love someone else more than you.[31]

SUGGESTED READINGS	SUGGESTED OCCASIONS
Acts 26:9–16	Community, parish meetings
1 Cor 13:1–13	Ordinary time
1 Pet 3:8–12	Catherine's feast— April 29

Catherine of Siena

(Theme—Prayer)

You see, then, perfect prayer is achieved not with many words but with loving desire, when the soul rises up to me with knowledge of herself, each movement seasoned by the other. In this way she will have vocal and mental prayer at the same time, for the two stand together like the active and contemplative life. Still, vocal and mental prayer are understood in many different ways. This is why I told you that holy desire, that is, having a good and holy will, is continual prayer. This will and desire rises at the appointed time and place to add actual prayer to the continual prayer of holy desire. So also with vocal prayer. As long as the soul remains firm in holy desire and will, she will make it at the appointed time. But sometimes, beyond the appointed times, she makes this continual prayer, as charity makes demands for her neighbors' good and according to the need she sees and the situation in which I have placed her.[32]

SUGGESTED READINGS	SUGGESTED OCCASIONS
2 Chr 6:18–21	Prayer days
Col 4:2–6	Ordinary time
	Catherine's feast—
	April 29

Catherine of Siena

(Themes—Humility, Penance)

Reprove yourself if ever the devil or your own short-sightedness should do you the disservice of making you want to force all my servants to walk by the same path you yourself follow, for this would be contrary to the teaching given you by my Truth. It often happens, when many are going the way of great penance, that some people would like to make everyone go that very same way. If everyone does not do so, they are displeased and scandalized because they think these others are not doing the right thing.

But you see how deluded they are, because it often happens that those who seem to be going wrong because they do less penance are actually better and more virtuous…than those who are doing the grumbling. This is why I told you earlier that if those who eat at the table of penance are not truly humble, and if their penance becomes their chief concern rather than an instrument of virtue, they will often, by this sort of grumbling, sin against their very perfection.[33]

Catherine of Siena

(Themes—Renewal, Baptism)

I, God, the eternal Trinity, in my infinite providence, saw to it that humankind was reclothed when you had lost the garment of innocence and were stripped of all virtue and perishing from hunger and dying from the cold in this life of pilgrimage....I, supreme providence, saw to this need of yours. Constrained not by any justice or virtue of yours but by my own goodness, I clothed you anew in the person of this gentle loving Word, my only-begotten Son. He, by stripping himself of life, clothed you anew in innocence and grace....

My providence provides for this not with bodily pain as was the custom in Old Testament circumcision, but with the gentleness of holy baptism. Thus have you been clothed anew. I made you warm again when my only-begotten Son revealed to you through his pierced body the fire of my charity hidden under the ashes of your humanity. And would this not warm the frozen human heart? Yes, unless it is so obstinate and blinded by selfishness that it does not see how unspeakably much I love you.[34]

SUGGESTED READINGS
Gal 3:23–29
Col 3:12–17

SUGGESTED OCCASIONS
Pentecost season
Community,
     parish meetings

Catherine of Siena

(Themes—Love, Friendship)

I have sent all of you into the vineyard of obedience to work in different ways. Each of you will be rewarded according to the measure of your love, not according to your work or the time spent. In other words, those who come early will not get more than those who come late, as it is said in the holy gospel. My Truth gave you the example of those who were standing idle and were sent by the Lord to work in His vineyard. He gave as much to those who went out at dawn as to those who went out at the first hour, as much as to those who went out at the third hour, the sixth, the ninth and near evening as to the first. My Truth was showing you that you are rewarded not according to your work or your time but according to the measure of your love. Many are sent in their childhood to work in this vineyard. Some enter later, and some even in their old age. These last sometimes, because they see how short a time they have, come in with such burning love that they catch up with those who enter in their childhood and have walked slowly. It is from the love of obedience, then, that the soul receives her merit; it is there she fills her vessel in me, the sea of peace.[35]

SUGGESTED READINGS
Isa 5:1–7

SUGGESTED OCCASIONS
Community,
     parish meetings

1 Cor 9:1–10

Ordinary time
Catherine's feast—
April 29

Dhuoda

written to her son, William, between 841–43

(Theme—Wisdom)

What shall I say, fragile vessel that I am? I shall turn to others as a friend. To be sure, if the heavens and the earth were spread through the air like a parchment, and if all various gulfs of the sea were transformed into ink, and if all the inhabitants of the earth born into this world from the beginning of humankind up to now were scribes—which is impossible—they would not be able to comprehend [in writing] the greatness, the breadth, the height, the sublimity, the profundity of the Almighty. Nor would they be able to tell of the divinity, wisdom, piety, and clemency of the one who is called God. Since God is so great that no one can comprehend the divine essence, I beg you to fear and to love God with all your heart, all your mind, all your understanding, to bless him in all your ways and deeds and to sing, "For God is good, his mercy endures forever!" Believe God to be above, below, inside and outside, for God is superior, inferior, interior and exterior.[36]

SUGGESTED READINGS
   Sir 42:15–25
   Isa 40:12–18, 21–23

SUGGESTED OCCASIONS
   Ordinary time
   Renewal days
   Feast of the Holy Trinity

Dhuoda

(Themes—Wisdom, Discernment)

Act according to the counsel of those who prepare you for faithful action in regard to your body and soul. It is written, "Do all things with counsel, and you shall not repent when you have done this." This "all things" does not include bad actions which destroy sane judgment, but rather higher and greater things which can lead without reprehension to the salvation of the soul and the body....

When those who work in metals begin to flatten gold to make leaves, they wait for a fitting and proper time, so that it may shine all the brighter with other shining metals. So, too, in the judgment of the prudent the consideration of reason must always be present. Indeed, the word of the prudent is whiter than snow, sweeter than honey, purer than gold or silver. Why? Because, as the Scriptures say, "From the mouth of the prudent proceeds honey. Good favor, as it were, is above silver and gold."

I also urge you not to neglect getting together, not only with the elders, but with the young who love God and seek wisdom. Old age derives its strength from youth. A certain one says, "The things that you have not gathered in your youth, how shall you find them in your old age?" You must seek wisdom from God saying, "Lord teach me from my youth; when I am old and gray-headed, do not forsake me. You will be blessed, my child, if you are taught by God and merit being learned in the divine law."[37]

SUGGESTED READINGS	SUGGESTED OCCASIONS
1 Tim 4:7–16	Ordinary time
Rule of Benedict,	Community,
chapters 3.1–6; 12–13	parish meetings
	Discernment days

Dhuoda

(Themes—Love, Service)

A certain learned one, making a comparison with a dumb animal for our edification, offered a great and clear sermon in a few words. He said the following in elucidating Psalm 41, "As the hart pants for running streams":

> Harts have this custom: when several of them wish to cross a sea or a large river of swirling waters, one after the other they place their horned heads on the back of their companions and hold up each other's necks, so that, by having a little rest, they can make a more rapid crossing. There is in them such intelligence and such wisdom that, when they perceive the first to be tired, they change places one after the other, letting the second be first, now upholding and comforting the others. Thus, changing one by one, each experiences the compassion of the other's love, always taking care that the head with the horns be shown and held up, lest they be submerged in the waters.

The meaning here is not hidden from the learned. In this upholding and in this changing of place is shown the love which is to be kept by all in the human race, both to the great and to the small through love. In the holding up of the heads and the horns is shown that the faithful in Christ must always keep their hearts and minds on Him.[38]

SUGGESTED READINGS	SUGGESTED OCCASIONS
Eph 4:7–16	Community,
Col 3:12–17	parish meetings
	Church Unity days
	Ordinary time

Dhuoda

(Themes—Perseverance, Suffering)

When I have ended my years, have my name listed among the honored dead. What I desire and what I beg you with all my power...is that in the place where I am buried, on the stone which covers the grave where my body is buried, you must have inscribed permanently the following verses, so that the people who see this epitaph will pray in a worthy fashion to God for me, so unworthy.

> Dhuoda's body, formed of earth,
> Lies buried in this tomb.
>   Immense King, receive her!
> Here the earth has received in its bowels
> The all too fragile clay which belonged to it.
>   Benign King, grant her pardon!
> Under and over her are the opaque depths
> Of the grave, bathed in her wounds.
>   O King, forgive her sins!
> O you of all ages and sexes who come
> And go here, I beg you, say this:
> Great *Hagios*, unlock her chains![39]
>   (N.B., *Hagios* is Greek for "holy")

SUGGESTED READINGS	SUGGESTED OCCASIONS
Gen 49:28–33	All Souls' Day
Col 2:9–15	Funerals

Egeria

(Theme—Hospitality)

At the fourth hour we arrived at the top of the holy mountain of God, Sinai, where the Law was given, in the place where the majesty of God descended on that day when the mountain of God smoked (Exod 19:18). Now in this place the summit of the mountain is not very large. Nonetheless the church itself is very graceful. When therefore by the help of God we had ascended to the height and arrived at the door of the church, there was the presbyter assigned to that church coming to meet us from his monastic cell. He was a healthy old man, and, as they say here, an "ascetic," and—what more can I say—quite worthy to be in this place. Then also other presbyters met us, and all the monks who live around the mountain, that is, if they were not prevented by age or weakness. In fact not one stays on the summit of the central mountain, for there is nothing there except the church and the cave where Saint Moses was (Exod 33:22).[40]

SUGGESTED READINGS	SUGGESTED OCCASIONS
Exod 19:16–21	Hospitality days
Exod 33:18–23	Ordinary time
Rule of Benedict, chapter 53.1–15	

Egeria

(Theme—Liturgy)

At one o'clock all of the people go up to Mount Olivet into the church: the bishop is seated; they sing hymns and antiphons appropriate to the day and place, as are the readings. When it is about three o'clock, they go down singing hymns to the place from which the Lord ascended into heaven, and everyone sits down there, for in the bishop's presence all the people are ordered to sit down. Only the deacons remain standing. Then hymns, antiphons and prayers are interspersed....That place in the Gospel is read where infants with palms and branches ran to the Lord, saying, "Blessed is he who comes in the name of the Lord" (Matt 21:9).

Immediately the bishop rises with all of the people and then they all walk from there to the summit of Mount Olivet. All the people walk before the bishop singing hymns and antiphons, always responding: "Blessed is he who comes in the name of the Lord." And whatever children in this place, even those not able to walk, are carried on their parent's shoulders, all holding branches, some of palm, some of olive; thus the bishop is led in the same way the Lord once was.[41]

SUGGESTED READINGS   **SUGGESTED OCCASIONS**
Rev 7:9–14   Holy Week
Eph 5:15–21   Palm Sunday

Egeria

(Theme—Baptism)

I should also write about the way those who are to be baptized at the Pasch are taught. Whoever gives his name, does so before the first day of Lent, and all the names are noted by the presbyters; this is before the start of those eight weeks which are, as I said, kept as the forty days. When all the names are noted by the presbyter, afterwards, on the next day of Lent, that which is the beginning of the eight weeks, the bishop's chair is placed in the middle of the great church, the Martyrium, and the priests sit on chairs and all the clergy stand about.

One by one the "competent" are led up; if they are men, with their fathers; if women, with their mothers. The bishop questions individually the neighbors of each who has come up, asking, "Is the person of good life? Respectful to parents? Not a drunkard or liar?" He also asks about the more serious vices in a person. If the person is proved without reproach in all of the things about which the bishop has questioned the witnesses present, he notes the person's name with his own hand. If, however, someone is accused of anything, the bishop immediately orders the person to leave, saying, "Change yourself, and if you do reform, come to the baptismal font." He makes such inquiries about both men and women. If, however, someone is a wanderer without witnesses who know the person, such a one will have a hard time being admitted to baptism.[42]

SUGGESTED READINGS	SUGGESTED OCCASIONS
Acts 8:9–17	Easter vigil
Jer 7:3–8	Pentecost season
	RCIA days

Elizabeth

(Themes—Trials, Suffering)

The sister of the holy bishop and martyr Paul was a deaconess named Elizabeth. She was in hiding in a house where the Christians had forcibly concealed her. On learning that the church was in flames, with the "members of the covenant" and the bones of her brother inside it, she dashed out of the house where the Christians had hidden her and went straight to the church, crying out, "I shall go to Christ with you, my brother, and with all the rest of you." This was what she was crying out as she reached the courtyard of the church, and when the people saw her there, they seized her, saying, "She has escaped from the fire, she has vanquished the fire by sorcery and got out!" But she assured them, "I haven't left the church—far be it; rather, I have come from outside in order to enter it and to be burnt along with the bones of my brother and with the priests, his companions. I want to be burnt in the church where I have ministered, together with my brother's bones." She was about forty-seven years old.[43]

SUGGESTED READINGS	SUGGESTED OCCASIONS
1 Pet 4:12–19	Feast of martyrs
Phil 1:27–30	Lent

Eudokia

(Themes—Suffering, Penance)

About nine in the evening the young woman [Justa] was singing about the good God. Suddenly she shivered to her core for she recognized the demon's presumptuousness, fanning a flame in her heart to divide her against herself. Swiftly, she thought of the Lord and prayed. She made the sign of the cross over everything in her room, and spoke eloquently, "Glorious God, Father of the spotless child Jesus Christ, and Master of all things, You who…save all those whom the monstrous snake takes alive in his snares; You who stretching forth Your hand to the starry heaven support the earth with its waters in the midst of the void; You who have…yoked the silvery moon to night; You who came to us in the form of a human who opened for us the abundance of heaven; You who recoiled from the advice of that most dreadful beast, the snake of the forest-covered earth; You Yourself sought our salvation, Lord, by Your merciful spirit, healing completely our injury with Your thorns, purifying all plans by the name of Christ....Come, save your servant by Your power...."

Having prayed this way, she armed herself with the sign of God, and drove away the disgusting demon through Christ's name. He sent the totally honorless demon flying.[44]

SUGGESTED READINGS	SUGGESTED OCCASIONS
Heb 3:1–6, 12–14	Feasts of virgins
Gen 3:8–15	Holy Name of Jesus
Dialogues of St. Gregory,	Lent
book II, chapter 3	Times of trial

Eudoxia

(Theme—Suffering)

But I suffer because, having wanted to stand in awe of God, I learned of the awesome death of the chilling monster and the emptiness of his courage, and am sunk in a dark morass myself. For I know that demons were completely impotent against the holy young virgin, the venerable Justa. I saw clearly that the scaly, intelligent, huge, puffed-up, mighty, terrible monster didn't have the power of even a single mosquito.

I learned of the Lord through the holy virgin, after I prayed a great deal, and did not run away from the truth. The young woman alone threw down under her feet so great a snake. That master of far-ranging idols did not dare approach the doorstep of the awesome virgin. He urged many spirits to attack her doors but none had power over the young woman. He who wished to rage over the earth yielded to a woman; he who had many cares in his heart could not overthrow her. Instead, the one who ate to excess like a lion called for aid and, like a mosquito, feared everything and prayed in front of her house.[45]

SUGGESTED READINGS	SUGGESTED OCCASIONS
1 Cor 10:14–21	Feast of virgins
Hab 1:4–11	Ordinary time

Gertrude of Helfta

(Themes—Wisdom, Spirituality)

When Gertrude found in Holy Scripture certain passages which she thought would be of use, if they seemed too difficult for persons of lesser intelligence, she would translate them into simpler language so that they might be of greater profit to their readers. She passed her life from morning to night with the sacred texts, either abridging long passages or explaining difficult ones, to the glory of God which she so much desired and for the salvation of others. The beauty of this work is well described by Bede: "What occupation more sublime or more pleasing to God could there be than to take one's daily study to convert others to the grace of their Creator and to add to the total number of the faithful souls ever increasing the joys of heaven?"[46]

SUGGESTED READINGS	SUGGESTED OCCASIONS
2 Tim 3:10–16	Gertrude's feast—
	November 16

Rom 15:1–6
Rule of Benedict,
   chapter 9.5–9

Renewal days
Ordinary time

Gertrude of Helfta

(Themes—Spirituality, Baptism)

One day between Easter and Ascension I went into the garden before Prime, and, sitting down beside the pond, I began to consider what a pleasant place it was. I was charmed by the clear water and flowing streams, the fresh green of the surrounding trees, the birds flying so freely about, especially the doves. But most of all, I loved the quiet, hidden peace of this secluded retreat. I asked myself what more was needed to complete my happiness in a place that seemed to me so perfect, and I reflected that it was the presence of a friend, intimate, affectionate, wise and companionable, to share my solitude.

And then you, my God...made me understand that, if I were to pour back like water the stream of graces received from you...; if, like a tree, growing in the exercise of virtue, I were to cover myself with the leaves and blossoms of good works (cf. Ps 1:3; Jer 17:8); if, like the doves (Ps 54:7) I were to spurn earth and soar heavenward; and if, with my senses set free from passions and worldly distractions, I were to occupy myself with you alone; then my heart would afford you a dwelling most suitably appointed from which no joys would be lacking.[47]

SUGGESTED READINGS
Gen 1:6–12
Col 3:12–17

SUGGESTED OCCASIONS
Spring/Easter time
Pentecost season
Ordinary time

Gertrude of Helfta

(Themes—Penance, Hospitality)

One evening I had given way to anger, and the next day, before dawn, I was taking the first opportunity to pray when you showed yourself to me in the guise of a pilgrim; as far as I could judge, you seemed to be destitute and helpless. Filled with remorse, with a guilty conscience, I bewailed my lapse of the previous day. I began to consider how unseemly it was to disturb you, Author of perfect purity and peace, with the turmoil of my wicked passions, and I thought it would be better—rather, I would actually prefer—to have you absent rather than present at such a time when I neglect to repel the enemy who was inciting me to do things so contrary to your nature.

This was your reply: "What consolation would there be for a sick person who, leaning on others, has just succeeded in going out to enjoy the sunshine when they are suddenly overtaken by a storm, had they not the hope of seeing clear sky again? In the same way, overcome by my love for you I have chosen to remain with you during the storm brought on by your sins to await the clear sky of your amendment in the shelter of your humiliation."[48]

SUGGESTED READINGS	SUGGESTED OCCASIONS
Ezra 18:26–32	Lent
Heb 6:1–8	Time of trial
	Ordinary time

Gertrude of Helfta

(Themes—Wisdom, Spirituality)

One day after washing my hands I was waiting with the community in the cloisters before going into the refectory, when I noticed the brightness of the sun, shining at the height of its noontide strength. Marveling, I said to myself: "If the Lord who created the sun, the Lord of whom it is said that the sun and the moon admire His beauty, and who is a consuming fire (Deut 4:24; Heb 12:29), is really united with my soul in the way which so often reveals God to me, how is it that I can treat others so coldly, so discourteously and even wickedly?"

And suddenly You, whose speech is always sweet (Song 4:3)... led me to infer this saying: "How would My infinite power be extolled if I did not reserve to Myself the power, in whatever place I might be, of keeping Myself to Myself, so that I might make Myself felt or seen only in the way that is most fitting according to places, times and persons? For from the beginning of the creation of heaven and earth, and in the whole work of the Redemption, I have employed wisdom and goodness rather than power and majesty. And the goodness of this wisdom shines forth best in my bearing with imperfect creatures till I draw them, of their own free will, into the way of perfection."[49]

SUGGESTED READINGS	SUGGESTED OCCASIONS
Heb 12:18–24	Renewal days
Deut 4:15–24	Gertrude's feast—
Sir 14:20–27	November 16
	Ordinary time

Gertrude of Helfta

(Themes—Virgin Mary, Prayer)

It was the hour of prayer and, coming into the presence of God, Gertrude asked what subject God would most like her to apply herself to during that hour. The Lord answered: "Keep close to my mother who is seated at my side, and strive to praise her." Then she devoutly hailed the Queen of heaven with the verse: "Paradise of pleasure"…praising her for having been the most pleasant abode which God's inscrutable wisdom…had chosen from all delectable pleasures.

She prayed that she might obtain for her own heart such attractive and varied virtues that God might be pleased to dwell there also. At that, the blessed Virgin seemed to bend down, as though to plant in the heart of the supplicant various flowers of virtue, such as the rose of charity, the lily of chastity, the violet of humility, the lilac of obedience and others of the same sort, showing by this how eager she always is to hear the prayers of those who call upon her.[50]

SUGGESTED READINGS	SUGGESTED OCCASIONS
Wis 7:7–14	Gertrude's feast—
Wis 7:22–30	November 16
	Feasts of Blessed Virgin
	Prayer days

Gertrude of Helfta

(Themes—Sacred Heart, Spirituality)

Another time, when she was striving to pay the greatest attention to each single note and word [in the music] and seeing that in this she was very often hindered by human frailty, sadly she said within herself: "And what profit can there be in a labor in which I am so inconsistent?" The Lord could not bear her sadness and gave her, with His own hands as it were, His divine heart in the form of a lighted lamp, saying: "Behold, here is My heart, the sweetest instrument of the ever adorable Trinity. I hold it in front of the eyes of your heart; it will supply all that you lack, faithfully making up for all that you entrust to it. And so everything will appear most perfect in My sight. Because, like a faithful servant who is always ready to do what God wants, from now on My heart will always cleave to you, so that it may make up at any time for all your negligences."[51]

SUGGESTED READINGS	SUGGESTED OCCASIONS
Eph 5:8–20	Feast of Sacred Heart
Judg 5:1–11	Gertrude's feast—
	November 16
	Ordinary time

Gertrude of Helfta

(Theme—Prayer)

Once as she was praying Gertrude asked the Lord what good it did her friends to pray for them all the time, while she saw in them no improvement as a result of her prayers. The Lord instructed her by this comparison: "When a child is brought back from the presence of a ruler who has enriched them with vast possessions and an immense revenue, which of those who look at the child can see any effect of what they have been given, although their future wealth and greatness are no secret from those who were witnesses? Do not be surprised, therefore, that you see no material result from your prayers, for I, in My eternal wisdom, will dispose of them in the most useful and perfect way. And no faithful prayer is without fruit, although the way in which it bears fruit is hidden from humankind."[52]

SUGGESTED READINGS	SUGGESTED OCCASIONS
1 Cor 13:4–13	Prayer days
2 Cor 5:2–10	Ordinary time
	Gertrude's feast—
	November 16

Hadewijch

(Themes—Humility, Discernment)

Be on your guard, therefore, and let nothing disturb your peace. Do good under all circumstances, but with no care for any profit, or any blessedness, or any damnation, or any salvation, or any martyrdom, but all you do or omit should be for the honor of Love. If you behave like this, you will soon be raised up again. Let people take you for a fool; there is much truth in that. Be docile and prompt toward all who have need of you, and satisfy everyone as far as you can manage it without disgracing yourself. Be joyful with those who rejoice, and weep with those who weep (Rom 12:13). Be good toward those who have need of you, devoted toward the sick, generous with the poor, and recollected in spirit beyond the reach of all creatures.

Even if you do the best you can in all things, your human nature must often fall short, so entrust yourself to God for God's goodness is greater than your failures. And always practice true virtues with confidence. Be diligent and constant in always following unconditionally our Lord's guidance and dearest will wherever you can discern it. Take care, doing your utmost to examine your thoughts strictly in order to know yourself in all things.[53]

SUGGESTED READINGS	SUGGESTED OCCASIONS
Rom 12:9–18	Ordinary time
Amos 5:4–8, 14–17	Renewal days
Sir 7:28–36	Communal penance

Hadewijch

(Themes—Love, Suffering)

I wish to put you on your guard this time against one thing from which much harm results. I tell you that, of all evils—which are still numerous everywhere—this is one of the most pernicious evils found among souls: everyone wishes to demand fidelity from others and to test their friend, while continually complaining on the subject of fidelity. These are the occupations we are now living in, when we ought to be tendering high love to the God of all greatness!

If we desire the good and wish to uplift our life in God's sublimity, why are we preoccupied about who treats us with fidelity or infidelity, or whether we should be thankful or reproachful toward one who does evil or good to us? The one who fails in fidelity or justice toward another is the one who suffers the greatest harm; and the worst of it is that that person often lacks the sweetness of fidelity.

If anyone, no matter who, behaves toward you with fidelity and helps you in the things you need, do not fail to thank them and to render them service in return; but serve and love God more heartily because someone is faithful, and as far as thanking or not thanking goes, leave that to God.[54]

SUGGESTED READINGS
Mal 2:8–12, 17
Gal 3:6–14

SUGGESTED OCCASIONS
Ordinary time
Advent
Lent

Hadewijch

(Themes—Love, Friendship)

First and above all I entreat you that you keep yourself from instability, for nothing could or can separate you from our Lord so quickly as instability. And do not be so self-willed in yourself at any unpleasantness that doubt or self-will makes you neglect any good action. Never let yourself doubt that, in the future, anything less than God totally shall be yours in the being of love. For if you abandon yourself to Love, you will soon attain full growth. And if you remain in doubt, you will become slothful and unwilling, so that everything you ought to do will be unwelcome to you. Do not be anxious about anything; and amid the tasks that lead to your goal, do not think there is anything so high that you cannot surely surmount it, or so remote that you cannot surely reach it. You must be ardent and persistent, with every new strength.[55]

SUGGESTED READINGS
1 John 4:9–18
Eph 4:1–6; 6:14–16

SUGGESTED OCCASIONS
Eucharistic feasts
Lent
Community, parish days

Hadewijch

(Themes—Love, Suffering)

When Christ lived on earth as a human being, all His works had their time (John 7:6). When the hour came (John 2:4) He acted; in words, in deeds, in preaching, in doctrine, in reprimands, in consolation, in miracles, and in penance; and in labors, in pains, in shame, in calumny, in anguish, and in distress, even to the passion, and even to death. In all these things He patiently awaited His time. When the hour came in which it befitted Him to act, He was intrepid and powerful in consummating His work; and He paid, by the service of perfect fidelity, the debt of human nature to the Divine Truth. Then "mercy and truth met together, and justice and peace kissed each other" (Ps 84:11).

With the Humanity of God you must live here on earth, in the labors and sorrow of exile, while within your soul you love and rejoice with the omnipotent and eternal Divinity in sweet abandonment. For the truth of both is one single fruition. And just as Christ's humanity surrendered itself on earth to the will of the Majesty, you must, with love, surrender yourself to both in unity. Serve humbly under their one power; stand always before them prepared to follow their will in its entirety and let them bring about in you whatever they wish.[56]

SUGGESTED READINGS	SUGGESTED OCCASIONS
Eccl 3:1–8	Lent
2 Cor 6:1–10	Discernment days
	Ordinary time

Hadewijch

(Themes—Penance, Suffering)

We all indeed wish to be God with God, but God knows there are few of us who want to live humanly with Christ's humanity, or want to carry His cross, or want to hang on the cross with Him and pay humanity's debt to the full….An unexpected sorrow, though slight, goes to our heart; or a slander, or a lie that people tell about us; or someone robs us of our honor or our rest or our own will. How quickly and deeply any of this wounds us! And we know so well what we want or do not want. There are so many things and kinds of things for which we have an attraction or an aversion: now alike, now different; now sweetness, now bitterness; now here, now there; now off, now on. In regard to everything, we are so ready to provide for ourselves if any rest for us is in sight!

This is why we remain unenlightened in our views, inconstant in our whole manner of acting, and unreliable in our reason and our understanding. We wander, poor and unhappy, exiled and robbed of everything on the rough roads of a foreign land (Luke 15:11–20). We all would have little need of doing so, were it not that illusions assail us on every side. By this we show plainly that we do not live with Christ as He lived; neither do we forsake all as Christ did, nor are we forsaken by all as Christ was….We do not live with Christ, and we do not carry the cross with the Son of God; rather, we carry it with Simon who received pay because he carried our Lord's cross (Matt 27:32).[57]

SUGGESTED READINGS	SUGGESTED OCCASIONS
Phil 1:18–26	Lent
Rom 2:18–29	Ordinary time
	Renewal days

Hadewijch

(Theme—Love)

Since I was ten years old I have been so overwhelmed by intense love that I should have died, during the first two years when I began experiencing this, if God had not given me other forms of strength than people ordinarily receive....God soon gave me reason, which was enlightened to some extent by many beautiful disclosures....Through them I experienced the presence and revelation of God's own Being. As is the custom of friends to hide little and reveal much between themselves, so through these manifestations, I met with God in an intimate exchange of love....These tokens which God, my Love, imparted to me in so many ways at the beginning of my life, gave me such confidence that ever since that time it has entered my mind that no one ever loved God so intensely as I.

In the meantime, reason made me understand that I was not the closest to God; nevertheless the chains of love that I felt never allowed me to feel or believe this. So that is how it is with me: though I do not, ultimately, believe God can be loved the most intensely by me, at the same time I also do not believe there is anyone living by whom God is loved so much. Sometimes Love so enlightens me that I know what is wanting in me—that I do not content my Beloved according to God's sublimity. But, at other times the sweet nature of Love blinds me to such a degree that when I can taste and feel Her it is enough for me; and sometimes I feel so rich in Love's presence that I myself acknowledge She contents me.[58]

SUGGESTED READINGS	SUGGESTED OCCASIONS
Song 2:8–17	Prayer days
Song 5:2–8	Feasts of women
Rule of Benedict,	Ordinary time
Prologue, 42–49	

Hadewijch

(Themes—Love, Friendship)

I will tell you without beating about the bush: be satisfied with nothing less than Love. Give reason its time, and always observe where you heed it too little and where enough. Do not let yourself be stopped by any pleasure through which your reason may be the loser. What I mean by "your reason" is that you must keep your insight ever vigilant in the use of discernment. Never must any difficulty hinder you from serving people, be they insignificant or important, sick or healthy. The sicker they are, and the fewer friends they have, the more readily must you serve them. Bear with foreigners willingly. As for all who slander you, contradict them not. And be desirous to associate with all who scorn you, for they make the way of Love broader for you.

Leave not anyone in need out of spite. Never fail to ask about any wise teaching you are ignorant of out of spite or shame that you do not know it. For you are bound before God to acquire a knowledge of all the virtues and to learn them by exertion, questioning and study, and earnest purpose. And if by your fault you have offended anyone, wait not too long to set it right with them. You are bound to this by the death of our Lord. Take whatever means you think the quickest and best to make peace with the one you have offended.[59]

SUGGESTED READINGS	SUGGESTED OCCASIONS
1 Cor 13:1–13	Ordinary time
Rule of Benedict,	Renewal days
chapter 4.59–74	

Hadewijch

(Theme—Love)

What is sweetest in Love is her tempestuousness;
Her deepest abyss is her most beautiful form;
To lose one's way in her is to touch her close at hand;
To die of hunger for her is to feed and taste;
Her despair is assurance;
Her sorest wounding is all curing;
To waste away for her sake is to be in repose;
Her hiding is finding at all hours;
To languish for her sake is to be in good health;
Her concealment reveals what can be known of her;
Her retentions are her gifts;
Wordlessness is her most beautiful utterance;
Imprisonment by her is total release;
Her sorest blow is her sweetest consolation;
Her ruthless robbery is great profit;
Her withdrawal is approach;
Her deepest silence is her sublime song;
Her greatest wrath is her dearest thanks;
Her greatest threat is pure fidelity;
Her sadness is the alleviation of all pain.[60]

SUGGESTED READINGS	SUGGESTED OCCASIONS
Song 2:1–7	Community days
Song 8:1–7	Feast of virgins

Hadewijch

(Theme—Love)

It seems to me that the commandment of love that God spoke to Moses is the weightiest I know in Scripture: "You shall love your Lord your God with all your heart, with all your soul, and with all your strength" (Deut 6:5). These words you shall never forget, sleeping or waking. If you sleep, you must dream of them; if you are awake, you must think of them, and recite them, and carry them into effect. These words you shall write…in all the places where you shall be, that you may not forget what you must do there (see Deut 6:6–9).

In other words, God commands that we nevermore forget Love, either sleeping or waking, in any manner with all that we are, with heart, with soul, with mind, with strength, and with our thoughts. God gave this commandment to Moses and in the Gospel (Matt 22:37; Mark 12:30; Luke 10:27), that in this way we should live wholly for Love.…How dare we then give Love short measure in anything?…Think about this, and work without neglect to promote Love above all things.[61]

SUGGESTED READINGS	SUGGESTED OCCASIONS
Deut 6:1–9	Community, parish days
Josh 22:1–6	Ordinary time
Rom 5:1–8	Discernment days

Hild of Whitby

(Themes—Love, Suffering)

When Hild had administered her monastery for many years, the blessed Author of our salvation subjected her holy soul to a long physical illness so that, like the apostle Paul, her strength might be made perfect in weakness. She was attacked by a fever which tortured her with its burning heat, and for six years she suffered continually from that sickness. During all this time, however, she never stopped giving thanks to her Maker and to instruct publicly and privately the flock committed to her charge. Taught by her own experience, she admonished them all, when health of body was given to them, to serve the Lord dutifully and, when in adversity or sickness, always to return thanks to the Lord faithfully.

In the seventh year of her illness Hild began to suffer internal pain and her last day arrived. About cock-crow she received the viaticum of the most holy Eucharist and then summoned the handmaidens of Christ who were in the monastery. She urged them to preserve the gospel peace among themselves and toward all others. While still exhorting them, she joyfully saw death approach or rather, to use the words of the Lord, she "passed from death into life."[62]

SUGGESTED READINGS	SUGGESTED OCCASIONS
2 Cor 12:1–10	Hild's feast— November 18
2 Cor 11:22–30	Times of trial, suffering

Hildegard of Bingen

(Theme—Pentecost)

From a letter to Bishop Eberhard II of Bamberg:

The Holy Spirit is like a fire, not one that can be extinguished, which suddenly bursts out in flames, and just as suddenly darkens. For the Holy Spirit streams through and ties together "eternity" and "equality" so that they are one. This is similar to someone tying a bundle together—for there would be no bundle if it weren't tied together; everything would fall apart. Or it is like a smith welding two pieces of metal together in a fire as one. It is like a circling sword swung in every direction.

The Holy Spirit bears witness to eternity, sets fire to equality, and so they are one. The Holy Spirit is in this eternity and equality; there God lives, the fire and life. The sun is brightly shining; its light flashes and the fire in it burns. It illuminates the whole world and appears as a unity. Everything in which there is no kind of power is dead, just as a branch cut off from a tree is dry because it has no greening power. The Holy Spirit is the firmness and aliveness.[63]

SUGGESTED READINGS	SUGGESTED OCCASIONS
Exod 3:1–6	Pentecost season
1 Thess 4:1–8	Community, parish days
1 Thess 5:9–19	Ordinary time

Hildegard of Bingen

(Theme—Stewardship)

From a letter to Archbishop Eberhard of Salzburg:

You who in your office represent the Son of the Living God, I see now that your situation resembles two walls joined together through one cornerstone. The one appears like a shining cloud; the other is somewhat shaded. And yet their situation is such that the brightness of the one doesn't affect the shadows; nor does the shadiness of the other mix with the light. The walls stand for your concerns, and these concerns meet in your spirit [the cornerstone]. For, on the one hand, your desires and feelings sigh for the narrow path that leads to God. But, on the other hand, you have a whole realm of worries about the people entrusted to you. The former is in light; the latter in shadow.

Your own desires are in the brightest light and you regard them as house guests, but this worldly concern lies in shadows and you look on it as an intruder. You don't allow yourself to see that they belong together and this is why you so frequently experience depression in your spirit. For you fail to see your striving for God and your concern for your people as a unity. And yet they both can be bound together as one....After all, Christ, too, adhered to heavenly things and yet at the same time He drew close to the people.[64]

SUGGESTED READINGS	SUGGESTED OCCASIONS
Acts 2:1–6	Pentecost
Num 9:15–23	Beginning a new undertaking
Eph 2:15–22	Community, parish days

Hildegard of Bingen

(Themes—Wisdom, Love)

From a letter to Bertha, Queen of Greece and Empress of Byzantium:

God's Spirit breathes and speaks: in wintertime, God takes care of the branch that is love. In summer, God causes that same branch to be green and to sprout with blossoms, removing diseased outgrowths that could do harm to the branch. It is through the little brook springing from stones in the east that other bubbling waters are washed clean, for it flows more swiftly. Besides, it is more useful than the other waters because there is no dirt in it.

These lessons also apply to every human being to whom God grants one day of the happiness and the glowing sunrise of glory. Such a person will not be oppressed by the strong north wind with its hateful foes of discord. So look to the One who has moved you and who desires from your heart a burnt offering, the gift of keeping all of God's commandments. Sigh for the Divine. And may God grant you what you desire and what you pray for in your need....The living eye of God looks on you: it wants to have you and you will live for eternity.[65]

SUGGESTED READINGS	SUGGESTED OCCASIONS
Gen 7:13–23	Beginning of winter/ summer
Prov 17:27–18:4	Ordinary time
	Feast of Hildegard— September 17

Hildegard of Bingen

(Theme—Stewardship)

From a letter to Abbot Withelo:

In the mirror of a true vision I saw you very agitated, similar to dangerous air which forms into a whirlwind by mixing with the current of a heavy rain-filled wind. This is how your thoughts are because your spirit is restless....

And I heard a voice and it was speaking about you:

A man is working on dry land with plow and oxen and he says to himself, "I cannot bear this work; it is too hard for me." And so he goes into an area without water and finds nonetheless that delicate flowers are growing there without any human effort. And yet these flowers are being stifled by weeds. And again the man says to himself: "I'll let the plow stand here for awhile and I'll pull out these weeds." What use is there in that? Now I want you to consider this: is this man more of a success when he works the land with the plow or when he works on pulling up the weeds that stifle the flowers?

I saw that the matter you aspire to is useless for you. Pull yourself together for the office that has been given you. Take hold of the plow. May God come to your aid in all your needs, and never let it happen that you sweat and strain for nothing.[66]

SUGGESTED READINGS	SUGGESTED OCCASIONS
Rom 14:12–19	Beginning of an
Heb 12:14–24	undertaking
	Ordinary time

Hildegard of Bingen

(Themes—Renewal, Discernment)

From a letter to an abbot:

Honorable father, from your love for God you have received me in your most inward compassion. I ask you for God's sake to listen to me, an unworthy serving-girl of the Divine. In regard to this monk, who because of his sins is longing to be taken into your fatherly mercy, I ask you to receive him. And give him counsel so that he doesn't destroy his body through unreasonable abstinence and end up fading away with weakness. Give him a moderate penance through which he can overcome the Devil who is seeking to outwit him.

He can do this with the help of your discretion, for discretion is a powerful mother who directs and orders all the virtues so that they are pleasing to God. For the old serpent hides itself in immoderate mortifications so that it can outwit and catch all those who strive after virtue without wise discernment. So you should bring this sheep as an offering to the almighty God, out of love for him who left the ninety-nine behind and placed on the divine shoulder the one who had gone astray. Hope in God, so that your striving may be like the burning sun and you might be a true servant of God and live in God's presence for eternity.[67]

SUGGESTED READINGS	SUGGESTED OCCASIONS
1 Chr 22:6–13	Communal penance
Prov 2:1–11	Discernment days
Rule of Benedict,	Ordinary time
chapter 27.1–6	

Hildegard of Bingen

(Themes—Renewal, Discernment)

Letter to Guibert of Gembloux:

From my infancy on, when my bones and nerves and veins were not yet strengthened, I have always seen this vision in my soul, up the present time when now I am more than seventy years old....

Whatever I see or learn in this vision, I retain as a memory for a long time, so that whenever I see or hear it I remember it. At the same time I see, hear, and know, and instantly learn what I know. But what I do not see, I do not know, since I am uneducated and have been taught only to read out letters in all simplicity. That which I write in the vision I see and hear; I do not set down any words other than those that I hear. I bring them forth in unpolished Latin just as I hear them in the vision, for in it I am not taught to write as the philosophers write. The words in the vision are not like the words that resound from the mouth of a human, but shine out like flames, and like clouds moving in the pure air.

In no way am I able to comprehend the form of this light, just as I cannot completely gaze upon the sphere of the sun. In this same light I once in a great while see another light, which I have been told is called the "Living light"; and when and how I am to see it I am unable to predict. But when I do see it, every sadness and every anxiety are lifted from me, so that I then feel like a simple maiden and not like an old woman.[68]

SUGGESTED READINGS	SUGGESTED OCCASIONS
2 Cor 12:1–9	Prayer days
Exod 34:27–35	Transfiguration
	Ordinary time
	Feast of Hildegard—
	September 17

Jane de Chantal
to her daughter, Countess de Toulonjon

(Theme—Prayer)

…upon awakening in the morning, turn your thoughts to God present everywhere; place your heart and your entire being in God's hands. Then think briefly of the good you will be able to accomplish that day and the evil you can avoid, especially by controlling your predominant fault. Resolve, by the grace of God, to do good and avoid evil. Then kneel down, adore God from the bottom of your heart and give thanks for all the benefits and graces that have been given to you. If you think about it for a moment you will realize how you have been surrounded by God's grace….This thought should touch your heart which you ought to offer God with all your good resolutions, affections, thoughts, words and deeds of that day, in union with our Divine Savior's offering of Himself on the tree of the cross. Ask Him for grace and assistance to guide you throughout the day….All this can be done in the space of two Paters and Aves; then get dressed quickly.[69]

SUGGESTED READINGS	SUGGESTED OCCASIONS
Rom 7:14–25	Days of prayer
1 Sam 12:18b–24	Days of thanksgiving
	Jane's feast—August 18
	Ordinary time

Jane de Chantal
to her brother, Archbishop of Bourges

(Theme—Prayer)

Every day in your morning exercise, or at the end of it, confirm your resolutions and unite your will with God's in all that you will do that day and in whatever the Divine One sends you. Use words like these:

> O most holy will of God, I give You infinite thanks for the mercy with which You have surrounded me. With all my strength and love, I adore You from the depths of my soul and unite my will to Yours now and forever, especially in all that I shall do and all that You will be pleased to send me this day, consecrating to Your glory my soul, my mind, my body, all my thoughts, words and actions, and my whole being. I beg You, with all the humility of my heart, accomplish in me Your eternal designs, and do not allow me to present any obstacle to this. Your eyes, which can see the most intimate recesses of my heart, know the intensity of my desire to live out Your holy will, but they can also see my weakness and limitations. That is why, prostrate before Your infinite mercy, I implore You, my Savior, through the gentleness and justice of this same will of Yours, to grant me the grace of accomplishing it perfectly, so that, consumed in the fire of Your love, I may be an acceptable holocaust which, with the glorious Virgin and all the saints, will praise and bless You forever.
>
> Amen.[70]

SUGGESTED READINGS
1 Chr 16:28–36
Heb 10:5–16
Eph 1:1–10

SUGGESTED OCCASIONS
Times of thanksgiving
Days of prayer
Ordinary time

Jane de Chantal
to her brother, Archbishop of Bourges

(Theme—Prayer)

As for prayer, don't burden yourself with making considerations; neither your mind nor mine is good at that. Follow your own way of speaking to our Lord sincerely, lovingly, confidently, and simply, as your heart dictates. Sometimes be content to stay ever so short a while in the Divine presence, faithfully and humbly, like a child before its parent, waiting to be told what to do, totally dependent on their will in which the child has placed all its love and trust. You may, if you wish, say a few words on this subject, very quietly: "You are my God from whom I expect all my happiness." A few moments later (for you must always wait a little to hear what God will say to your heart): "I am your child, all yours; good children think only of pleasing their parent; I don't want to have any worries and I leave in your care everything that concerns me, for you love me, my God. You are my good. My soul rests and trusts in your love and eternal providence." Try to let yourself be penetrated by words like these.[71]

SUGGESTED READINGS
1 Tim 4:4–10
Exod 33:12–20

SUGGESTED OCCASIONS
Days of prayer
Ordinary time
Jane's feast—August 18

Jane de Chantal

to a religious, Marie-Aimess de Morville

(Theme—Spirituality)

Praised be forever the Divine Savior who has seen fit to cast a ray of holy light into your soul! Only God can enlighten us and open our blind eyes. My daughter, if your passions hadn't taken over, you could have perished through vanity and self-love. It seems to me that for your own happiness, it was necessary that you fall into that bottomless pit toward which you were racing. All the human knowledge in the world would not have been enough to draw you away from your illusions. But with great mercy, God took care of you. For the rest of your life you ought to be deeply prostrate before God, and very humble and docile toward others. Let yourself be guided, without resistance, and love the humiliations that keep you humble. May God grant you this grace. And, imperfect as I am, I am the most devoted, loving friend that you have. I ask God...to sanctify you, as well as all our dear sisters whom I greet with affection.

As to the complaints you make to me about yourself, dear, the cause may be in your own tendency to be slow and put things off. So long as you are careful to direct your intention to do all for God, then you need only have courage and be gentle with yourself in all your frailty.[72]

SUGGESTED READINGS	SUGGESTED OCCASIONS
Eph 1:15–21	Discernment times
1 Cor 1:25–31	Community, parish days
	Ordinary time
	Jane's feast—August 18

Jane de Chantal

to Sister Peronne-Marie de Chatel

(Themes—Spirituality, Prayer)

No matter what happens, be gentle and patient with yourself. Once in a while, if you feel particularly weak, without courage, without confidence, force yourself to make affirmations which are the opposite of your feelings. Say with conviction: "My Savior, my All, despite my feelings of misery and distrust, I place all my confidence in You; You are strength for the weak, refuge for the miserable, wealth for the poor; You are indeed my Savior who has always loved sinners." But dearest [Peronne], say these or similar words resolutely, without self-pity or tears; then turn your attention to something else. The Almighty will never let you slip from the Divine arms which hold you firmly. Don't you see how very gently God comes to your rescue?[73]

SUGGESTED READINGS	SUGGESTED OCCASIONS
1 Cor 4:14–21	Prayer days
Col 3:12–17	Ordinary time

Jane de Chantal

to Sister Peronne-Marie de Chatel

(Themes—Renewal, Discernment)

…my darling Peronne, once again I am asking you to cheer up our dear Sister and to keep an eye on her health. Without nagging her, do tell her frankly what she should do to stay well. See to it that she follows through on what you tell her. She should yield to your request in this, just as you should obey her quite simply when she orders what she considers necessary for your health. You may correct her humbly, but in such a manner that she will not lose confidence in you and be unhappy; it is better to be too lenient than to work her too hard. And don't be overly anxious about your own problems. Do whatever you can to get well, for it is only your nerves.

I am closing now because I do not feel well. A thousand million greetings to all our darling Sisters. I certainly love that little flock with all my heart. I want them to be ever attentive to their Spouse and to live in God's presence like pure, sweet, simple and chaste doves. In spirit I embrace them all lovingly and tenderly—everyone, young and old....[74]

SUGGESTED READINGS	SUGGESTED OCCASIONS
Exod 23:20–26	Community days
Prov 18:4–14	Ordinary time
Rule of Benedict,	Jane's feast—August 18
chapter 36.1–6, 10	

Jane de Chantal
to Mother Jenne-Charlotte de Brechard

(Themes—Renewal, Discernment)

You do well, daughter, to humble your soul under the hand of God and to accept lovingly humiliations and contradictions as suited to our littleness and nothingness. Dearest, while you have the opportunity, I beg you, do try to become truly humble, gentle, and simple, so that your dear heart which I love so tenderly may become a real heart of Jesus.

You are right, it is not wise to reprimand the Sisters for every little fault. The mind grows weary of that and gets so used to it that gradually it becomes insensitive to correction. When you need to correct someone, it is better to put it off a little and make the correction in private and with kindness.

No one should be permitted, under pretext of their charge, to go poking about the house. The Superior and the Procuratrix have that responsibility. Poor Sister M. Avoye especially does not need that freedom. You must let her finish out her year and help her to keep up her courage. She's terribly sensitive, and yet she's very good.[75]

SUGGESTED READINGS	**SUGGESTED OCCASIONS**
2 Tim 4:1–8	Community, parish days
Prov 15:1–12	Ordinary time
Rule of Benedict,	
chapter 27.5–9	

Jane de Chantal
to Mother Peronne-Marie de Chatel

(Themes—Renewal, Discernment)

We must show great respect to the confessors and do all we can reasonably to satisfy them, honoring God in them. However, we must not be subject to them in procuring preachers, having Masses said, receiving holy communion from persons of repute or others whom we may want to please, or to confess ourselves to such persons when it seems suitable. In all such matters you must remain very free, for such decisions rest completely with you. This is what the Rule and our customs specify. And just as we must, with prudence and discernment, make use of the holy liberty that is given us, so we must guard it carefully and jealously, but always with humility. We show these confessors due respect, yet we explain to them very frankly our liberty of action.[76]

SUGGESTED READINGS	SUGGESTED OCCASIONS
1 Cor 9:18–27	Communal penance
Gal 5:1, 13–18	Community, parish days
	Ordinary time

Jane de Chantal
to the Sisters of the Visitation at Annecy

(Theme—Spirituality)

Since our Lord, in his goodness, has gathered our hearts into one, allow me, my dearest Sisters, to greet you all, as a community and individually; for this same Lord will not allow me to greet you in any other way. But what a greeting it is! The very one that our great and worthy Father [Francis de Sales] taught us: "LIVE JESUS!" Yes, my beloved Sisters and daughters, I say the words with intense delight: "LIVE JESUS" in our memory, in our will, and in all our actions! Have in your thoughts only Jesus, in your will have only the longing for His love, and in your actions have only obedience and submission to His good pleasure by an exact observance of the Rule, not only in externals, but, much more, in your interior spirit: a spirit of gentle cordiality toward one another, a spirit of recollection of your whole being before our divine Master, and that true, sincere humility which makes us as simple and gentle as lambs.[77]

SUGGESTED READINGS	SUGGESTED OCCASIONS
Phil 2:2–11	Feasts of Jesus
2 Cor 4:5–14	Community, parish days
	Ordinary time
	Jane's feast—August 18

Jane de Chantal

to Mother Paule-Jeronyme

(Themes—Renewal, Discernment)

Our corrections should always be firm and serious, yet they should be made gently and humbly, never sharply....My dear, I think God wanted me to write this, for I hadn't thought about it beforehand, as it is off the subject of the misunderstanding between you and that Sister....Win her by gentleness but without giving in to her whims which are contrary to the spirit of your house. Patience, dear! I am very pleased that you aren't becoming discouraged. I realize that you are somewhat brusque by nature. Fight against that and try, with God's help, to govern gently and graciously. You will see that all the Sisters advance more joyously and faithfully. I have greatly recommended you to God during these special days, dearest daughter, you and your little flock whom I greet affectionately.[78]

SUGGESTED READINGS	SUGGESTED OCCASIONS
Heb 12:5–13	Community, parish days
Prov 13:1, 9–11	Ordinary time
	Jane's feast—August 18
	Days of prayer

Jane de Chantal

to Sister Anne-Marie Rosset

(Themes—Renewal, Discernment)

I am convinced, and experience has taught me, that nothing so wins souls as gentleness and cordiality.…Curtness in words or actions only hardens hearts and depresses them, whereas gentleness encourages them and makes them receptive.…I suggest this strongly in the case of Sister Anne Jacqueline who has to be handled playfully. She is still very much a child and wouldn't have the stomach for eating solid meat, so to speak, and whoever would give her some would ruin her. She has to be led slowly and tenderly, and be brought to observe silence and other obediences, but not as yet to perform penances and mortifications. You see, my dear, we have to cultivate in these young, delicate souls lots of vigor, cheerfulness, and joy, and thus bring them to want those things they would fear or dread if they were led in any other manner.[79]

SUGGESTED READINGS	SUGGESTED OCCASIONS
Heb 5:11–14; 6:1–3	Days of prayer
Prov 15:11–15, 29–33	Ordinary time
Rule of Benedict,	Jane's feast—August 18
chapter 27.1–9	

Jane de Chantal

to the superior at Digne

(Themes—Renewal, Discernment)

In the name of our Divine Savior, I beg you, and urge you, to govern according to the Spirit and that of our vocation, which is a humble, gentle spirit, supportive and considerate of all. In order to govern in this manner, you must not act according to the willfulness of your own nature, nor according to your inclination to austerity. What we are asking of you, my dearest daughter, and without further delay, please, is to be most gentle in spirit, word and action, and to treat your own body and those of your Sisters better than you have been doing.

What good will it do to put bread on the table when they don't have teeth to chew it or stomachs to digest it? So, I urge you once again not to let us hear any more talk about your harshness and severity with the Sisters and yourself. Your minds and bodies will be wrecked if you stubbornly refuse to accept humbly what we are saying and begging you to do in the name of God and of our blessed Father [Francis de Sales]. He greatly feared such harshness in his Institute, which he established for those who are delicate and where he wanted a spirit of humility and gentleness to reign.[80]

SUGGESTED READINGS	SUGGESTED OCCASIONS
1 Thess 5:12–22	Lent
Eph 4:23-32	Days of prayer
	Ordinary time
	Jane's feast—August 18

Jane de Chantal
to the novice mistress at Grenoble

(Theme—Spirituality)

It seems to me, my dear Sister, that you should try to make your own devotion, and that of the novices, generous, noble, straightforward, and sincere. Try to foster that spirit in all those whom God will ever commit to your care—a spirit founded on that deep humility which results in sincere obedience, sweet charity which supports and excuses all, and an innocent, guileless simplicity which makes us even-tempered and friendly toward everyone.

From there, my dearest daughter, move on to a total surrender of yourself into the hands of our good God, so that, insofar as you can, you may help your own dear soul and those you are guiding, to be free of all that is not God. May these souls have such a pure, upright intention that they do not waste time worrying about created things—their friends, their appearance, their speech. Without stopping at such considerations or at any other obstacle they may meet along the way, may they go forward on the road to perfection by the exact observances of the Institute, seeing in all things on the sacred face of God.[81]

SUGGESTED READINGS	SUGGESTED OCCASIONS
Titus 2:11–3:1–5	Days of prayer
2 John 2:1–7	Ordinary time
	Jane's feast—August 18

Jane de Chantal
to the superior at Rumilly

(Themes—Penance, Detachment)

Dearest, here is the money for the new habit which you sent me, and please, send me back the one which our Sisters kept. There is nothing that bothers me more than their attachment to these external signs of imaginary holiness in me. These are traps which the devil puts in my way to make me stumble into the bottomless pit of pride. I am already weak enough, and enough of a stumbling-block to myself, without anyone adding another. So I beg all of you not to be an occasion of such temptation for me. If anyone has anything belonging to me, do me the kindness of burning it. If only our Sisters would treat me as I deserve to be treated before God, then I would have some hope of becoming, through these humiliations, what they imagine me to be. But to be presenting me with continual temptations to vanity is intolerable. This brings sadness to my heart and tears to my eyes as I tell it to you.[82]

SUGGESTED READINGS	SUGGESTED OCCASIONS
1 Cor 3:10–23	Days of prayer
Heb 2:10–18	Ordinary time
	Jane's feast—August 18

Jane de Chantal
to a Visitation community

(Themes—Love, Spirituality)

May you all live in harmony with one heart and mind in God. Do not wish for anything except what your superiors and your Sisters ask of you. Show a childlike trust and gentleness toward one another, supporting each one in mutual charity. Never be astonished at the faults of the community or of any individual Sister, for to be shocked at our Sisters' faults, to pick them apart, examine them, to get all upset about them is the sign of a narrow-mindedness which has no insight into human frailty, and very little charity or forbearance. That is why those who are inclined to be so righteous should close their eyes to what is going on around them and remind themselves constantly that charity does not go looking for evil, and when she does come upon it, she looks the other way and excuses those who commit it. This should be our attitude toward our Sisters who are our companions.[83]

SUGGESTED READINGS
Rom 12:9–21
Prov 25:18–23

SUGGESTED OCCASIONS
Community, parish days
Ordinary time
Jane's feast—August 18

Jane de Chantal
to a Visitandine

(Themes—Penance, Spirituality)

Your letter showed me very clearly, the state of your soul and the source of its pain and perplexity, which is your over eagerness to attain the true happiness you desire, and your lack of patience and docility to the will of the One who alone can grant it to you. Therefore, if you really want to acquire the spirit of your vocation, you will have to correct this over eagerness. Do everything you are taught in a spirit of gentleness and fidelity in order to reach the goal toward which you are being guided, cutting short all thought of attaining it except in God's good time.

It seems to me that you are not satisfied with doing those acts required for your perfection, but that you want to feel and know that you are doing them. You must put an end to that and be content with telling God, without any feeling, "Lord, with all my heart I desire to practice such and such virtue just to please You." Then, set to work, although without feeling, and lovingly resolve to serve God in this way, desiring nothing more. If you do this, you will soon find yourself in that state of tranquility and peace which is so necessary for souls who wish to live virtuously, according to the spirit, not according to their own inclinations and judgments.[84]

SUGGESTED READINGS	SUGGESTED OCCASIONS
Jer 7:22–28	Days of prayer
Col 3:1–11	Ordinary time
	Jane's feast—August 18

Jane de Chantal
to a superior

(Theme—Love)

I beg you, my dear Sister, govern your community with great expansiveness of heart: give the Sisters a holy liberty of spirit, and banish from your mind and theirs a servile spirit of constraint. If a Sister seems to lack confidence in you, don't for that reason show her the least coldness, but gain her trust through love and kindness. Don't entertain thoughts against any one of the Sisters, but treat them all equally. Lead them, not with a bustling, anxious kind of concern, but with a care that is genuine, loving and gentle. I know no better way to succeed in leading souls. The more solicitous, open, and supportive you are with them, the more you will win their hearts. This is the best way of helping them advance toward the perfection of their vocation. Be present at the community exercises as often as you can, and let the Sisters know how much you enjoy being with them.[85]

SUGGESTED READINGS   SUGGESTED OCCASIONS
Rom 8:5–13   Jane's feast—August 18
1 Cor 12:18–26   Ordinary time

Julian of Norwich

(Themes—Creation, Providence)

God showed me something small, no bigger than a hazelnut, lying in the palm of my hand, and I perceived that it was as round as any ball. I looked at it and thought: *What can this be?* And I was given this general answer: "It is everything which is made." I marveled that it could last, for I thought that it was so little that it could suddenly fall into nothing. And I was answered in my understanding: "It lasts and always will, because God loves it; and thus everything has being through the love of God."

In this little thing I saw three truths. The first is that God made it. The second is that God loves it. The third is that God preserves it. But what is that to me? It is that God is the Creator and the lover and the protector. For until I am one with God I can never have love or rest or true happiness; until, that is, I am so attached to God there is no created thing between my God and me.[86]

SUGGESTED READINGS   SUGGESTED OCCASIONS
Gen 1:16–25   Julian's feast—May 8
Deut 4:32–39   Prayer days
    Ordinary time

Julian of Norwich

(Theme—Mary)

God brought our Lady to my understanding. I saw her spiritually in her bodily likeness—a simple, humble maiden, young in years, of the stature which she had when she conceived. God showed me also part of the wisdom and truth of her soul, so that I understood the reverent contemplation with which she beheld her God, marveling with great reverence that God was willing to be born of her who was a simple creature that God had made. This wisdom and truth, this knowledge of her Creator's greatness and of her own created littleness, made her say humbly to Gabriel, "Behold God's handmaid." In this sight I saw truly that she is greater, more worthy and more fulfilled than anything else which God has created. No created thing is above her, except the blessed humanity of Christ.[87]

SUGGESTED READINGS	SUGGESTED OCCASIONS
Prov 3:25–34	Feasts of Mary
Job 22:21–30	Ordinary time

Julian of Norwich

(Themes—Faith, Confidence)

…our Lord very humbly revealed words to me, without voice and without opening of lips, as He had done before, and said very seriously: Know it well, it was no hallucination which you saw today, but accept and believe it and hold firmly to it, and you will not be overcome. These last words were said to me to teach me perfect certainty that it is our Lord Jesus who revealed everything to me; for just as in the first words which our Lord revealed to me, alluding to His blessed Passion: "With this the fiend is overcome," just so He said with perfect certainty in these last words: "You will not be overcome" ....And these words: "You will not be overcome," were said very insistently and strongly, for certainty and strength against every tribulation which may come. He did not say: "You will not be assailed, you will not be overstressed, you will not be disquieted," but He said: "You will not be overcome." God wants us to pay attention to His words, and always to be strong in our certainty, in well-being and in woe, for He loves us and delights in us, and so He wishes us to love Him and delight in Him and trust greatly in Him, and all will be well.[88]

SUGGESTED READINGS	SUGGESTED OCCASIONS
John 16:29–33	Time of trial or stress
Jer 1:15–19	Beginning a project

Julian of Norwich

(Theme—Providence)

I saw truly that God does everything, however small it may be and that nothing is done by chance, but all by God's discerning wisdom. If it seems like chance in our sight, it is because of our blindness and lack of discernment. For those things in God's foreseen wisdom since before time—which God always guides to their best conclusion—come upon us suddenly, so that in our blindness we say that they are chance.

So I understood in this revelation of love...that in God's sight there is no chance; and therefore I was compelled to admit that everything which is done is well done, for all is done by God.[89]

SUGGESTED READINGS	SUGGESTED OCCASIONS
Eccl 3:1–11	Beginning of a project
Job 10:2–12	Ordinary time
	Julian's feast—May 8

Julian of Norwich

(Themes—Thanksgiving, Prayer)

Thanksgiving belongs to prayer. Thanksgiving is a true inward acknowledgment, we applying ourselves with great reverence and loving fear with all our powers to the work that God moved us to, rejoicing and giving thanks inwardly. Sometimes the soul is so full of this that it breaks out in words and says: "Good Lord, great thanks, blessed may You be." And sometimes the heart is dry and feels nothing, or else, by the temptation of our enemy, reason and grace drive us to implore our Lord with words, recounting His blessed Passion and great goodness. And so the power of the Lord's word enters the soul and enlivens the heart and…makes us pray most blessedly and truly to rejoice in our Lord. This is the most loving thanksgiving in God's sight.[90]

SUGGESTED READINGS	SUGGESTED OCCASIONS
Col 3:12–17; 4:2	Thanksgiving Day
Phil 4:1–9	Feasts of Jesus
	Ordinary time

Julian of Norwich

(Themes—Love, Friendship)

I saw very truly that all our endless friendship, our place, our life and our being are in God. For that same endless goodness which protects us when we sin so that we do not perish, that same endless goodness constantly draws into us a peace, opposing our wrath and our perverse falling, and makes us see our need with true fear, and urgently to beseech God that we may have forgiveness, with a grace-given desire for our salvation. For we cannot be blessedly saved until we are truly in peace and in love, for that is our salvation.[91]

SUGGESTED READINGS	SUGGESTED OCCASIONS
Heb 6:1–9	Easter season
1 Pet 2:1–10	Ordinary time
	Julian's feast—May 8

Julian of Norwich

(Themes—Love, Spirituality)

In this endless love we are led and protected by God, and we never shall be lost; for God wants us to know that the soul is a life, which life of goodness and grace will last in heaven without end, loving God, thanking God, praising God. And just as we were to be without end, so we were treasured and hidden in God, known and loved from without beginning. Therefore God wants us to know that the noblest thing ever made is humankind, and the fullest substance and the highest power is the blessed soul of Christ. And, furthermore, God wants us to know that this beloved soul was preciously knitted in its making, by a knot so subtle and so mighty that it is united in God. In this uniting it is made endlessly holy. Furthermore, God wants us to know that all the souls which will be saved in heaven without end are knit in this knot, and united in this union, and made holy in this holiness.[92]

SUGGESTED READINGS	SUGGESTED OCCASIONS
Col 3:1–11	Easter season
1 John 1:1–7	Feasts of Jesus
Eph 1:15–23	Ordinary time

Julian of Norwich

(Themes—Wisdom, Spirituality)

I saw no difference between God and our substance, but, as it were, all God; and still my understanding accepted that our substance is in God, that is to say that God is God, and our substance is a creature in God. For the almighty truth of the Trinity is our Father, for He made us and keeps us in Him. And the deep wisdom of the Trinity is our Mother, in whom we are enclosed. And the high goodness of the Trinity is our Lord, and in Him we are enclosed and he in us. We are enclosed in the Father, and we are enclosed in the Son, and we are enclosed in the Holy Spirit. And the Father is enclosed in us, the Son is enclosed in us, and the Holy Spirit is enclosed in us, almighty, all wisdom and all goodness, one God, one Lord.[93]

SUGGESTED READINGS	SUGGESTED OCCASIONS
Eph 3:16–21; 4:1–6	Feast of Holy Trinity
1 Cor 15:21–28	Ordinary time
	Julian's feast—May 8

Julian of Norwich

(Themes—Love, Motherhood of God)

Jesus is our true Mother in nature by our first creation, and He is our true Mother in grace by His taking our created nature. All the lovely works and all the sweet loving offices of beloved Motherhood are appropriated to the second person, for in Him we have this godly will, whole and safe forever, both in nature and in grace, from His own goodness proper to Him.

I understand three ways of contemplating Motherhood in God. The first is the foundation of our nature's creation; the second is His taking of our nature, where the Motherhood of grace begins; the third is the Motherhood at work. And in that, by the same grace, everything is penetrated, in length and in breadth, in height and in depth without end; and it is all one love.[94]

SUGGESTED READINGS	SUGGESTED OCCASIONS
Isa 49:8–16	Feasts of Jesus
Isa 66:7–13	Christmas season
	Ordinary time

Julian of Norwich

(Themes—Compassion, Love)

A mother may sometimes suffer the child to fall and to be distressed in various ways, for its own benefit, but she can never suffer any kind of peril to come to her child because of her love. And though our earthly mother may suffer her child to perish, our heavenly Mother Jesus will never suffer us who are

His children to perish, for Jesus is almighty, all wisdom, and all love....

But when our falling and our wretchedness are shown to us we are so much afraid and so greatly ashamed of ourselves that we scarcely know where to put ourselves. But our courteous Mother does not wish us to flee away....Jesus wants us to behave as a child who, when it is distressed and frightened, runs quickly to its mother; and if it can do no more, it calls to the mother for help with all its might. So Jesus wants us to act as a meek child, saying: My kind Mother, my gracious Mother, my beloved Mother, have mercy on me. I may not and cannot make things right except with Your help and grace.[95]

SUGGESTED READINGS	SUGGESTED OCCASIONS
Exod 19:3–8	Communal penance
Isa 49:13–18	Renewal days
Rom 7:14–25	Feasts of Jesus

Julian of Norwich

(Theme—Perseverance)

I have understood two contraries. One is the wisest act which any creature can perform in this life, the other is the most foolish. The wisest act is for everyone to do according to the will and counsel of their greatest friend. This blessed friend is Jesus and it is His will and counsel that we keep with Him and fasten ourselves closely to Him in whatever state we may be. For whether we be foul or clean, we are always the same in His love; for well or for woe, He wants us never to flee from him.

But because of our own inconstancy we often fall into sin. Then by the prompting of our enemy and our own folly and blindness we come to this. They say, "You know well that you are a wretch, a sinner and unfaithful because you do not keep your covenant. You are always promising our Lord you will do better, and then you fall again into the same state, especially into sloth and wasting of time." That, as I see it, is the beginning of sin, especially for those who have given themselves to serve our Lord by the inward contemplation of the Divine goodness.[96]

SUGGESTED READINGS	SUGGESTED OCCASIONS
Isa 42:10–18	Communal penance
Eccl 2:11–17	Renewal days
	Julian's feast—May 8

Leoba

(Theme—Love)

The girl [Leoba] grew up and was taught with such care by the abbess and all the nuns that she had no interest other than the monastery and the pursuit of sacred knowledge. She took no pleasure in aimless jests and wasted no time on girlish romances, but, fired by the love of Christ, fixed her mind always on reading or hearing the Word of God. Whatever she heard or read she committed to memory, and put all that she learned into practice....She prayed continually, knowing that in the Epistles the faithful are counseled to prayer without ceasing (1 Thess 5:17). When she was not praying she worked with her hands at whatever was commanded her, for she had learned that the one who will not work should not eat (2 Thess 3:10).

However, she spent more time in reading and listening to Sacred Scripture than she gave to manual labor. She took great care not to forget what she had heard or read, observing the commandments of the Lord and putting into practice what she remembered of them. In this way she so arranged her conduct that she was loved by all the sisters. She learned from all and obeyed them all, and by imitating the good qualities of each one she modeled herself on the continence of one, the cheerfulness of another; copying here a sister's mildness, there a sister's patience. One she tried to equal in attention to prayer, another in devotion to reading. Above all, she was intent on practicing charity, without which, as she knew, all other virtues are void.[97]

SUGGESTED READINGS	SUGGESTED OCCASIONS
1 Thess 5:12–24	Labor Day
2 Thess 3:4–12	Leoba's feast—
	September 28
	Ordinary time

Leoba

(Theme—Wisdom)

Leoba…had a dream in which she saw a purple thread issuing from her mouth. It seemed to her that when she took hold of it with her hand and tried to draw it out there was no end to it; and as if it were coming from her very bowels, it extended little by little until it was of enormous length. When her hand was full of thread and it still issued from her mouth, she rolled it round and round and made a ball of it.…Now there was in the same monastery an aged nun who was known to possess the spirit of prophecy. [Leoba sent one of her sisters to the nun for an interpretation]:

The thread which came from her bowels and issued from her mouth signifies the wise counsels she will speak from her heart. The fact that it filled her hand means that she will carry out in her actions whatever she expresses in her words. Furthermore, the ball which she made by rolling it round and round signifies the mystery of the divine teaching, which is set in motion by the words and deeds of those who give instruction and which turns earthwards through active works and heavenwards through contemplation—at one time swinging downwards through compassion for one's neighbor, again swinging upwards through the love of God. By these signs God shows that your mistress will profit many by her words and example, and the effect of them will be felt in other lands afar....[98]

SUGGESTED READINGS	SUGGESTED OCCASIONS
Wis 7:7–15	Discernment days
1 Kgs 3:4–14	Ordinary time
	Leoba's feast—
	September 28

Leoba

(Theme—Discipleship)

At the time when the blessed virgin Leoba was pursuing her quest for perfection in the monastery, the holy martyr Boniface was being ordained by Gregory, Bishop of Rome and successor to Constantine in the apostolic See. His mission was to preach the Word of God to the people of Germany. When Boniface found that the people were ready to receive the faith and that, though the harvest was great, the laborers who worked with him were few, he sent messengers and letters to England, his native land, summoning from different ranks of the clergy many who were learned in the divine law and fitted both by their character and good works to preach the Word of God.

Likewise, he sent messengers with a letter to the abbess Tetta...asking her to send Leoba to accompany him on this journey and to take part in this embassy; for Leoba's reputation for learning and holiness had spread far and wide and her praise was on everyone's lips. The abbess Tetta was exceedingly displeased at her departure, but because she could not gainsay the dispositions of divine providence she agreed to his request and sent Leoba to the blessed man....When she came, the man of God received her with the deepest reverence, holding her in great affection, not so much because she was related to him on his mother's side as because he knew that by her holiness and wisdom she would confer many benefits by her word and example.[99]

SUGGESTED READINGS	SUGGESTED OCCASIONS
Esth 2:8–17	Leoba's feast—
1 Sam 15:13–23	September 28
	Feasts of women
	St. Boniface's feast—
	June 5

Leoba

(Themes—Discipleship, Stewardship)

Boniface appointed persons in authority over the monasteries; he placed Sturm as abbot over the monks and Leoba as abbess

over the nuns....These were trained according to her princi-
ples in the discipline of monastic life and made such progress
in her teaching that many of them afterwards became superiors of others, so that there was hardly a convent of nuns in
that part which had not one of her disciples as abbess. She was
a woman of great virtue and was so strongly attached to the
way of life she had vowed that she never gave thought to her
native country or her relatives. She expended all her energies
on the work she had undertaken in order to appear blameless
before God and to become a pattern of perfection to those
who obeyed her in word and action. She was ever on her
guard not to teach others what she did not carry out herself.
In her conduct there was no arrogance, or pride; she was no
distinguisher of persons, but showed herself affable and kindly
to all. In appearance she was angelic, in word pleasant, clear in
mind, great in prudence, catholic in faith, most patient in
hope, universal in her charity. But though she was always
cheerful, she never broke out into laughter through excessive
hilarity. No one ever heard a bad word from her lips; the sun
never went down upon her anger.[100]

SUGGESTED READINGS	SUGGESTED OCCASIONS
1 Tim 4:4–10	Leoba's feast—
	September 28
Rule of Benedict,	Feasts of women
chapter 2.7–15	
Rule of Benedict,	St. Boniface's feast—
chapter 4.52–74	June 5

Leoba

(Themes—Discipleship, Stewardship)

Leoba was held in veneration by all who knew her, even by kings. Pippin, King of the Franks, and his sons Charles and Carloman treated her with profound respect, particularly Charles who...after some years, took over the reins of government....Many times he summoned the holy virgin to his court, received her with every mark of respect and loaded her with gifts suitable to her station. Queen Hiltigard also revered her with a chaste affection and loved her as her own soul. She would have liked her to remain continually at her side so that she might progress in the spiritual life and profit by her words and example. But Leoba detested the life at court like poison. The princes loved her, the nobles received her, the bishops welcomed her with joy. And because of her wide knowledge of the Scriptures and her prudence in counsel they often discussed spiritual matters and ecclesiastical discipline with her. But her deepest concern was the work she had begun. She visited the various convents of nuns and, like a mistress of novices, stimulated them to vie with one another in reaching perfection.[101]

SUGGESTED READINGS	SUGGESTED OCCASIONS
1 Pet 2:11–17	Leoba's feast— September 28
Rom 13:1–10	Feasts of women
Rule of Benedict, chapter 72	Ordinary time

Leoba

(Theme—Service)

Leoba took leave of the Queen with these words, "Farewell for evermore, my dearly beloved lady and sister; farewell, most precious half of my soul. May Christ our Creator and Redeemer, grant that we shall meet again without shame on the day of judgment. Never more on this earth shall we enjoy each other's presence."

So Leoba returned to the convent, and after a few days she was stricken by sickness and was confined to her bed. When she saw that her ailment was growing worse and that the hour of her death was near, she sent for a saintly English priest who had always been at her side and ministered to her with respect and love, and received from him the viaticum of the body and blood of Christ. She died in the month of September, the fourth of the kalends of October. Her body, followed by a long cortege of noble persons, was carried by the monks of Fulda to their monastery with every mark of respect. Thus the seniors there remembered what Saint Boniface had said, namely, that it was his last wish that her remains should be placed next to his bones. They buried her on the north side of the altar which the martyr Saint Boniface had himself erected and consecrated in honor of our Savior and the twelve Apostles.[102]

SUGGESTED READINGS	SUGGESTED OCCASIONS
Jas 5:13–20	Leoba's feast— September 28
Acts 28:1–10	Feasts of women
Rule of Benedict, chapter 36	Ordinary time

Margery Kempe

(speaking of her own experience)

(Theme—Penance)

Then on a Friday before Christmas Day, as this creature, kneeling in Saint John's chapel within the church of Saint Margaret in Lynn, wept wondrously, asking mercy and forgiveness of her sins and her trespasses, our merciful Lord Christ Jesus—blessed may He be—ravished her spirit and said to her:

> Daughter, why do you weep so painfully? I am come to you, Jesus Christ, who died on the cross suffering bitter pains and passions for you. I, the same God, forgive you your sins completely. You will never come into hell or into purgatory, but, when you pass out of this world, within the twinkling of an eye you shall have the bliss of heaven, for I am the same God who brought your sins to your mind and made you to be freed from them. I grant you contrition until the end of your life. Therefore, I bid you and command you, boldly call me Jesus, your love, for I am your love and shall be your love without end. Daughter, you have a haircloth upon your back. I will that you put it away and I shall give you a haircloth in your heart that shall please me much better than all the haircloths in the world.[103]

SUGGESTED READINGS
  1 John 1:5–10; 2:1–2
  Col 3:1–4, 12–17

SUGGESTED OCCASIONS
  Prayer days
  Lent
  Ordinary time

Marguerite Porete

(Theme—Love)

Charity obeys no created thing except Love. Charity has nothing of her own, and if she possesses anything, she never says that it is hers. Charity leaves her own work and goes to do that of others. Charity asks no return from any creature for whatever good deed or favor she does. Charity has neither shame, nor fear, nor sickness; she is so righteous that she cannot yield, whatever may happen.

Charity neither does nor cares for anything under the sun; all the world is her relief and her due. Charity gives to all what she has of value; she never withholds herself and often promises what she does not have in her great generosity, hoping that for the one who gives, more remains. Charity is such a wise merchant that where others lose, she makes a profit. She escapes the bonds with which others bind themselves and therefore has a great abundance of what pleases Love. And note that who would have perfect charity is mortified in the affections of the life of the spirit by the action of charity.[104]

SUGGESTED READINGS	SUGGESTED OCCASIONS
2 Cor 9:6–15	Social justice days
Gal 6:2–10	Community days
	Marguerite's feast—June 1

Martha

(Themes—Suffering, Service)

They led the chaste virgin Martha off on the Sunday of the great feast of Christ's resurrection, at midday. As they were getting ready the place where she was to be put to death, she fell down on her face and, as she knelt before God facing east, she said,

> I thank you, Jesus Christ, my Lord, my King and my Betrothed, for preserving my virginity sealed up with the imprint of the seal-ring of your promise, and for preserving my faith in the glorious Trinity—the faith in which I was born, in which my parents brought me up, and in which I was baptized. For this confession, for which my father Posi was also crowned, I give you thanks, O Lamb of God who takes away the sin of the world, for whose sake the bishops, our shepherds, have been sacrificed, as have the head pastors, the priests, and along with them the members of the holy covenant; and slaughtered, too, have been the sheep....And now it is the turn for me, the young lamb who has been fattened up on the pastures of your promises and by the springs of your declarations; here I am being sacrificed before you. At your hands, Jesus, the true High Priest, may I be offered up as a pure, holy, and acceptable offering....Visit, Lord, your persecuted people; preserve them in true faith in the midst of their enemies, and may they be found to be like pure gold in the furnace of persecution...; may they be strengthened in the worship of your majesty, fearlessly worshipping and confessing Father, Son, and Holy Spirit, now and always and for eternal ages, amen.[105]

SUGGESTED READINGS	SUGGESTED OCCASIONS
Rom 8:28–39	Feasts of martyrs
2 Tim 3:1–12	Feasts of women
Rule of Benedict,	Time of trial
chapter 7.35–41	

Martha

(Theme—Suffering)

The moment Martha had finished her prayer, while no one was near at hand, she rushed off and stretched herself on the ground above the pit they had dug for her. When the officer approached to tie her up, she said, "Do not tie me up for I am gladly accepting immolation for the sake of my Lord." When she saw the knife being brandished by the officer, she laughed and said, "Now I can say, not like Isaac, 'Here is the fire and the wood, but where is the lamb for the burnt offering?' but rather I can say, 'Here is the lamb and the knife, but where are the wood and the fire?' But I do have wood and fire, for the wood is the cross of Jesus my Lord, and I do have fire too— the fire that Christ left on earth, just as he said, 'I came to cast fire on earth; I only wish it had already caught alight!'"

The thousands of spectators who stood by were astounded at the chaste girl's courage, and everyone gave praise to the God who encourages those who fear God in this way. The officer then approached and slaughtered her like a lamb, while she entrusted her soul to Christ.[106]

SUGGESTED READINGS	SUGGESTED OCCASIONS
Gen 22:1–8	Feasts of martyrs
Heb 11:13–19	Feasts of virgins
Acts 20:17–27	Ordinary time

Mechtild of Magdeburg

(Theme—Spirituality)

What hinders spiritual people most of all from complete perfection is that they pay so little attention to small sins. I tell you in truth: when I hold back a smile which would harm no one, or have a sourness in my heart which I tell to no one, or feel some impatience with my own pain, then my soul becomes so dark and my senses so dull and my heart so cold that I must weep greatly and lament pitiably and yearn greatly and humbly confess all my lack of virtue—for only then can I receive the blessing of being allowed to crawl back to the kitchen like a beaten dog. Moreover, if I have not recognized and changed a flaw in myself, there is at once an evil mark on my soul.

No one can comprehend divine gifts with human senses; therefore those persons err who do not keep their spirit open to unseen truth. What can be seen with the eyes of the flesh, heard with the ears of the flesh, and spoken with the mouth of the flesh is as different from the truth revealed to the loving soul as a candle to the bright sun.[107]

SUGGESTED READINGS	SUGGESTED OCCASIONS
2 Cor 4:6–18	Renewal days
1 Cor 2:6–16	Prayer days
	Ordinary time
	Mechtild's feast—
	November 19

Mechtild of Magdeburg

(Theme—Prayer)

This is the way a beggar woman speaks to God in prayer:

Lord, I thank You that since with Your love You have taken from me all earthly riches; You now clothe and feed me out of the goodness of others, for all that once clothed my heart in the desire of possession has become foreign to me.

Lord, I thank You that since You have taken from me the power of my eyes, You now serve me through the eyes of others.

Lord, I thank You that since You have taken from me the power of my hands...and since You have taken from me the power of my heart, You now serve me with the hands and hearts of others.

Lord, I ask You to reward them here on earth with Your divine love so that they might beseech and serve You with all virtues until they come to a holy end.[108]

SUGGESTED READINGS	SUGGESTED OCCASIONS
Col 3:12–17	Ordinary time
1 Pet 5:1–10	Social justice days
	Days of prayer
	Mechtild's feast—
	November 19

Mechtild of Magdeburg

(Themes—Suffering, Spirituality)

Not long after I came to the convent I became so painfully ill that my attendants had great pity for me. Then I spoke to our Lord: "What do you want with this suffering?" And our dear Lord said this: "All your paths are measured, all your footsteps counted, your life is blessed, your end will be happy, and my kingdom is very near you."

"Lord, why is my life blessed, since I can do so little good?" Then our Lord said: "Your life is sanctified because my rod has never left your back!"[109]

SUGGESTED READINGS	SUGGESTED OCCASIONS
1 Pet 4:12–19	Lent
1 Pet 1:6–13	Ordinary time
	Mechtild's feast—
	November 19

Mechtild of Magdeburg

(Theme—Penance)

I, poor woman, was so bold in my prayer that I impudently took corrupt Christianity into the arms of my soul and lifted it in lamentation. Our Lord said: "Leave it! It is too heavy for you."

"No, sweet Lord! I will lift it up and carry it before Your feet, with Your own arms with which you bore it on the cross! And God granted me, poor wretch, my will that I might find rest."

When poor Christianity came before our Lord, she was like a maiden. I looked at her and saw also that our Lord looked at her. And I was very ashamed. Then our Lord said: "Behold, is it fitting for me to love this maid in my eternal infinite wedding bed and to draw her to me in my regal arms and to look at her with my divine eyes, since she is half-blind in her knowledge and crippled in her hands which hardly do any good works? She also limps in the feet of her desire, for she rarely, and even then, indolently thinks of me. Her skin is also filthy, for she is unclean and unchaste."

Then the poor soul spoke: "What advice can one give her?" And our Lord said: "I will wash her in my own blood and I will protect all the blessed who are truly innocent and take them intimately to me in a blessed death...."[110]

SUGGESTED READINGS	SUGGESTED OCCASIONS
Rev 7:9–17	All Saints' Day
Exod 12:21–28	All Souls' Day
Rev 14:6–16	Lent
	Feasts of the church

Mechtild of Magdeburg

(Themes—Liturgy, Spirituality)

The throne of God and heaven form together a noble dwelling which encloses the void and the nine choirs....

> Of all these things I can speak but a brief word,
> no more than as much
> honey as a bee can
> carry away on its foot from a full hive.
> In the first choir is happiness,
> the highest of all gifts,

in the second choir is meekness,
in the third choir is love,
in the fourth sweetness; in the fifth joyfulness,
in the sixth noble tranquility,
in the seventh riches,
in the eighth worthiness,
in the ninth burning love,
and in the sweet beyond is pure holiness....[111]

SUGGESTED READINGS	SUGGESTED OCCASIONS
Rev 19:5–10	All Saints' Day
Rev 4:1–11	Easter season
	Trinity Sunday
	Mechtild's feast—
	November 19

Mechtild of Magdeburg

(Themes—Hospitality, Stewardship)

Power is dangerous. When someone says: "you are now our prelate or our prior or our prioress," God knows, dear monk, you have been chosen for the highest....You should be lovingly cheerful or gently serious with your subordinates and you should be compassionate....

Even though you are master or mistress
you are subordinate to them.
You should not stay too long with the guests
for you should diligently see to the convent.
The guests should not keep long watches,
for that is a sacred thing.

You should go to the infirmary every day
and anoint the sick with comforting words of God
and delight them generously with earthly things,
for God is rich above all price.
...if you stand truly by them,
God's sweetness will flow into you.
You should also go to the kitchen and see to it
that their provisions are good enough
that your thriftiness and the cook's laziness
may not rob our Lord
of sweet song in choir!
For a hungry person never sings well
and a hungry person cannot study deeply.
Thus might God often lose the best because of the
least.[112]

SUGGESTED READINGS	SUGGESTED OCCASIONS
Rom 13:1–7	Election time
Rule of Benedict,	Ordinary time
chapter 2.1–12	Mechtild's feast—
	November 19

Mechtild of Magdeburg

(Themes—Humility, Stewardship)

Beware of arrogant thoughts which unfortunately come into
the heart under the guise of good and say: "Yes, you are prior
or prioress over them all; you can indeed do what you deem
good...." When the brethren or sisters of your house offer
you honor, you should fear inwardly with a sharp guard on
your heart and outwardly be modest with proper behavior.

You should receive all complaints with compassion and give advice in good faith....Have an eagle eye and view those under you in God, lovingly, not angrily. If you find anyone who is secretly tempted, stand by them with all your love....

Now, dear friend, there are still two things against which you must be on your guard with holy diligence, for they have never brought holy fruit. The first is that men or women devoted to good works and practices will do much in order to be chosen superior. This brings grief to my soul. If such persons come to power, their vices become so manifold that none of those who chose them will receive comfort. Their honors will become a reproach and their false virtues will be converted to vices. The second thing to guard against is, if someone without sin is laudably chosen and then changes so much that they never wish to give up their elected office, this, too, is a sign of many false virtues.[113]

SUGGESTED READINGS	SUGGESTED OCCASIONS
1 Thess 5:12–22	Days of renewal
2 Tim 4:1–5	Ordinary time
	Mechtild's feast—
	November 19

Mechtild of Magdeburg

(Themes—Humility, Love)

> The abbess is true love,
> she has much holy sense
> with which she watches over the community
> in body and soul to the glory of God;
> she gives them many holy teachings

as to what is the will of God.
By this her own soul becomes free.
The chaplain of love is divine humility,
which is always so subordinate to love
that pride must stand aside.
The prioress is the holy peace of God;
patience is given to her goodwill
so that she may teach the community with divine
    wisdom....
The subprioress is lovingness.
She shall gather together the small sins
and destroy them with godliness....[114]

SUGGESTED READINGS	SUGGESTED OCCASIONS
Rom 13:1–8	Election time
Rule of Benedict, chapter	Ordinary times
2.30–36 or 65.1–6,	Mechtild's feast—
11–13	November 19

Mechtild of Magdeburg

(Themes—Love, Spirituality)

Lord, my earthly nature is stood before my eyes
like a barren field
which hath few good plants grown in it.
Alas, sweetest Jesus and Christ,
now send me the sweet rain of thy humanity
and the hot sun of thy living Godhead
and the gentle dew of the holy Spirit
that I may wail and cry out the aches of my heart.[115]

SUGGESTED READINGS	SUGGESTED OCCASIONS
2 Cor 12:1–10	Mechtild's feast—November 19
2 Cor 13:1–8	Time of trial

Olympias

(Theme—Spirituality)

The Kingdom of our Savior Jesus Christ, existing before the ages and shining forth to ages without end, confers immortality on those who have served as its shield-bearers, who have completed the race and kept their faith in God spotless and steadfast. Among them was Thecla, a citizen of heaven, a martyr who conquered in many contests, the holy one among women, who despised wealth and the transitory pleasures of this world. Having followed the teachings of Paul, the blessed apostle, and having taken into her heart the divinely inspired Scriptures, she received the crown of incorruptibility from our Lord and Savior Jesus Christ and to ages without end she rests with all the saints who from eternity have pleased the Lord Jesus Christ. Olympias walked in the footsteps of this saint, Thecla, in every virtue of the divinely-inspired way of life. Olympias, most serious and zealous for the road leading to heaven, followed the intent of the divine Scriptures in everything and was perfected through these things. She was daughter, according to the flesh, of Seleucus, one of the city assembly members, but according to the spirit, she was the true child of God.[116]

SUGGESTED READINGS	SUGGESTED OCCASIONS
2 Tim 4:1–8	Olympias' feast—
	December 16
Gal 2:15–21	Feast of women-martyrs

Olympias

(Themes—Love, Service)

One was struck with amazement at seeing certain things in the holy chorus and angelic institution of these holy women: the constancy of their praise and thanksgiving to God, their *charity which is the bond of perfection* (Col 3:14), their stillness. For no one from the outside, neither man nor woman, was permitted to come upon them, the only exception being the most holy patriarch John [Chrysostom], who visited continuously and sustained them with his most wise teachings. The pious and blessed Olympias [who, in these matters, too, imitated the disciples of Christ who served him from their possessions] prepared for the holy John his daily provisions and sent them to the bishop, for there was not much separation between the episcopal residence and the monastery, only a wall. And she did this not only before the plots against him, but also after he was banished; up to the end of his life, she provided for all his expenses as well as for those who were with him in his exile.[117]

SUGGESTED READINGS	SUGGESTED OCCASIONS
Col 3:12–17	Feasts of women
1 Tim 6:11–19	Social justice days
	Olympias' feast—
	December 16

Olympias

(Themes—Love, Service)

I have deemed it necessary and entirely useful for the profit of many to run over in the narrative one by one the holy virtues of the noble servant of God, Olympias, who is among the saints. For no place, no country, no desert, no island, no distant setting, remained without a share in the benevolence of this famous woman; rather, she furnished the churches with liturgical offerings and helped the monasteries and convents, the beggars, the prisoners, and those in exile; quite simply, she distributed her alms over the entire inhabited world. And the blessed Olympias herself burst the supreme limit in her almsgiving and her humility, so that nothing can be found greater than what she did. She had a life without vanity, an appearance without pretense, character without affectation, a face without adornment; she kept watch without sleeping, she had a mind without vainglory, intelligence without conceit, an untroubled heart, an artless spirit, charity without limits, unbounded generosity, contemptible clothing, immeasurable self-control, rectitude of thought, undying hope in God, ineffable almsgiving; she was the ornament of all the humble and was in addition worthily honored by the most holy patriarch John [Chrysostom].[118]

SUGGESTED READINGS	SUGGESTED OCCASIONS
2 Cor 8:1–7	Social justice days
2 Cor 8:8–15	Feasts of women
	Olympias' feast—
	December 16

Perpetua

(Themes—Suffering, Service)

While I was still with the police authorities my father, out of love for me, tried to dissuade me from my resolution. I said, "Father, do you see here, for example, this vase or pitcher, or whatever it is?" He responded, "I see it." I asked, "Can it be named anything else than what it really is?" He said, "No." Then I said, "So I also cannot be called anything else than what I am, a Christian."

A few days later we were imprisoned. I was terrified because never before had I experienced such darkness. What a terrible day! Because of the crowded conditions and rough treatment by the soldiers the heat was unbearable. My condition was aggravated by my anxiety for my baby. Then the kind deacons Tertius and Pomponius, who were taking care of our needs, paid for us to be moved for a few hours to a better part of the prison where we might refresh ourselves. Leaving the dungeon we all went about our own business. I nursed my child, who was already weak from hunger. In my anxiety for the infant I spoke to my mother about him, tried to console my brother, and asked that they care for my son. I suffered intensely because I sensed their agony on my account. These were the trials I had to endure for many days. Then I was granted the privilege of having my son remain with me in prison. Being relieved of my anxiety and concern for the infant, I regained my strength. Suddenly the prison became my palace, and I loved being there rather than any other place.[119]

SUGGESTED READINGS	SUGGESTED OCCASIONS
Gen 39:20–23; 40:1–8	Perpetua's feast— March 7
Acts 12:1–11	Feast of virgin-martyrs
Col 4:2–12	Lent

Perpetua

(Themes—Love, Suffering)

A few days later there was a rumor that our case was to be heard. My father, completely exhausted from his anxiety, came from the city to see me, with the intention of weakening my faith. *Daughter,* he said, "Have pity on my grey head. Have pity on your father if I have the honor to be called father by you. If with these hands I have brought you to the prime of your life, and if I have always favored you above your brothers, do not abandon me to the reproach of others. Consider your brothers; consider your mother and your aunt; consider your son who cannot live without you. Give up your stubbornness before you destroy all of us. None of us will be able to speak freely if anything happens to you."

These were the things my father said out of love, kissing my hands and throwing himself at my feet. With tears he called me not *daughter,* but *woman.* I was very upset because of my father's condition. He was the only member of my family who would find no reason for joy in my suffering. I tried to comfort him saying, "Whatever God wants at this tribunal will happen, for remember that our power comes not from ourselves but from God." But utterly dejected, my father left me.[120]

SUGGESTED READINGS	SUGGESTED OCCASIONS
Job 2:1–10	Martyrs' feasts
Gen 37:3–11	Perpetua/Felicitas—
	March 7
	Vocation/Formation days

Perpetua

(Themes—Love, Suffering)

As for Felicitas, she too was touched by God's grace in the following manner. She was pregnant when arrested, and was now in her eighth month. As the day of the contest approached she became very distressed that her martyrdom might be delayed, since the law forbade the execution of a pregnant woman. Then she would later have to shed her holy and innocent blood among common criminals. Her friends in martyrdom were equally sad at the thought of abandoning such a good friend to travel alone on the same road to hope.

And so, two days before the contest they prayed to the Lord. Immediately after the prayers her labor pains began. Because of the additional pain natural for an eighth-month delivery, she suffered greatly during the birth, and one of the prison guards taunted her: "If you're complaining now, what will you do when you'll be thrown to the wild beasts? You didn't think of them when you refused to sacrifice." She answered, "Now it is I who suffer, but then another shall be in me to bear the pain for me, since I am now suffering for him." And she gave birth to a girl whom one of her sisters reared as her own daughter.[121]

SUGGESTED READINGS	SUGGESTED OCCASIONS
Mic 4:6–13	Felicitas/Perpetua— March 7
2 Cor 6:1–10 Acts 7:51–60	Feasts of martyrs

Perpetua

(Themes—Love, Spirituality)

We add an instance of Perpetua's perseverance and lively spirit. At one time the prisoners were being treated with unusual severity by the commanding officer because certain deceitful people had suggested to him that the prisoners might escape through some kind of magic. Perpetua openly challenged him: "Why don't you at least allow us to freshen up, the most noble of the condemned, since we belong to Caesar and are about to fight on his birthday? Or isn't it to your credit that we should appear in good condition on that day?" The officer grimaced and blushed, then ordered that they be treated more humanely and that her brothers and others be allowed to visit and dine with them. By this time the prison warden was himself a believer.

On the day before the public games, as they were eating the last meal commonly called the "free meal," they tried as much as possible to make it instead an agape. In the same spirit they were exhorting the people, warning them to remember the judgment of God, asking them to be witnesses to the prisoners' joy in suffering, and ridiculing the curiosity of the crowd. Saturus told them, "Won't tomorrow's view be enough for you? Why are you so eager to see something you hate? Friends today, enemies tomorrow! Take a good look so you'll recognize us on that day." Then they all left the prison amazed, and many of them began to believe.[122]

SUGGESTED READINGS	SUGGESTED OCCASIONS
Acts 16:23–34	Martyr saints
Acts 12:1–11	Perpetua's feast—March 7
1 Pet 2:18–25	

Perpetua

(Theme—Suffering)

The day of their victory dawned. With joyful countenances they marched from the prison to the arena as though on their way to heaven. If there was any trembling, it was from joy, not fear. Perpetua followed with quick step as a true spouse of Christ, the darling of God, her brightly flashing eyes quelling the gaze of the crowd. Felicitas too, joyful because she had safely survived child-birth and was now able to participate in the contest with the wild animals, passed from one shedding of blood to another; from midwife to gladiator, about to be purified after child-birth by a second baptism.

As they were led through the gate they were ordered to put on different clothes: the men, those of the priests of Saturn, the women, those of the priestesses of Ceres. But that noble woman stubbornly resisted even to the end. She said, "We've come this far voluntarily in order to protect our rights, and we've pledged our lives not to recapitulate on any such matter as this. We made this agreement with you." Injustice bowed to justice and the guard conceded that they could enter the arena in their ordinary dress. Perpetua was singing victory psalms as if already crushing the head of the Egyptian.[123]

SUGGESTED READINGS	SUGGESTED OCCASIONS
Exod 23:23–33	Perpetua/Felicitas—
Acts 5:21b–32	March 7
1 Pet 4:12–19	Martyrs' feasts
Col 1:22–29	Lent-Holy Saturday
	RCIA liturgies

Perpetua

(Themes—Love, Suffering)

Whoever said, "Ask and you shall receive," granted to these petitioners the particular death that each one chose. For whenever the martyrs were discussing among themselves their choice of death, Saturus used to say that he wished to be thrown in with all the animals so that they might wear a more glorious crown. Accordingly, at the outset of the show he was matched against a leopard but then called back; then he was mauled by a bear on the exhibition platform.

Saturus detested nothing as much as a bear and he already decided to die by one bite from the leopard. Consequently, when he was tied to a wild boar, the professional gladiator who had tied the two together was pierced instead and died shortly after the games ended, while Saturus was merely dragged about. When he was tied up on the bridge in front of the bear, the bear refused to come out of his den; and so a second time Saturus was called back unharmed.[124]

SUGGESTED READINGS	**SUGGESTED OCCASIONS**
Jas 1:2–7, 12–13	Martyrs' feasts
2 Tim 2:1–12	Time of trial

Perpetua

(Themes—Suffering, Service)

For the young women, a mad cow was readied, an animal not usually used at these games, but selected so that the women's sex would be matched with that of the animal….Perpetua was tossed first and fell on her back. She sat up, and being more concerned with her sense of modesty than with her pain, covered her thighs with her gown which had been torn down one side. Then finding her hair-clip which had fallen out, she pinned back her loose hair thinking it not proper for a martyr to suffer with disheveled hair: it might seem that she was mourning in her hour of triumph. She stood up and, noticing that Felicitas was badly bruised, she went to her, reached out her hands and helped her to her feet. As they stood there the cruelty of the crowds seemed to be appeased. They were sent to the Sanavivarian Gate where Perpetua was taken care of by a certain catechumen, Rusticus, who stayed near her.

She seemed to be waking from a deep sleep so completely had she been entranced and imbued with the Spirit. She began to look around her and to everyone's astonishment asked, "When are we going to be led out to that cow, or whatever it is?" She would not believe that it had already happened until she saw the various markings of the tossing on her body and clothing. Then calling for her brother she said to him and to the catechumen, "Remain strong in your faith and love one another. Do not let our excruciating sufferings become a stumbling block for you."[125]

SUGGESTED READINGS	SUGGESTED OCCASIONS
Dan 14:23–32	Martyrs' feasts
2 Cor 1:3–11	Perpetua/Felicitas—
	March 7
	Lent

Perpetua

(Themes—Suffering, Service)

Meanwhile, at another gate Saturus was similarly encouraging the soldier, Pudens. "Up to the present," he said, "I've not been harmed by any of the animals, just as I foretold and predicted. So that you will now believe completely, watch as I go back to die from a single leopard bite." And so, at the end of that contest, Saturus was bitten once by the leopard that had been set loose, and bled so profusely from that one wound that, as he was coming back, the crowd shouted in witness to his second baptism: "Salvation by being cleansed; salvation by being cleansed...."

Then Saturus said to Pudens the soldier, "Goodbye, and remember my faith. Let these happenings be a source of strength for you, rather than a cause of anxiety." Then, asking Pudens for a ring from his finger, he dipped it into the wound and returned it to Pudens as a legacy, a pledge and remembrance of his death. And as he collapsed he was thrown with the rest to the place reserved for the usual throat-slitting. When the crowd demanded that the prisoners be brought out into the open so that they might feast their eyes on death by the sword, they voluntarily arose and moved where the crowd wanted them. Before doing so they kissed each other so that their martyrdom would be completely perfected by the rite of the kiss of peace.[126]

SUGGESTED READINGS	SUGGESTED OCCASIONS
1 John 5:1–11	Martyrs' feasts
Acts 22:17–24	Lent
	Easter (baptism)

120

Proba

(Themes—Environment, Stewardship)

And now the second day was rising with the earliest morning star. The earth poured forth flowers unfolding all her foliage and the wild haunts of birds blushed with blood-red berries; not subject they to hoes or other human care.

The third day had removed from heaven the cool shade. Then the distant thickets resounded with melodious birds and ravens with narrowed throats sent forth their liquid songs; nor did the turtledove cease cooing from its airy elm.

On the fourth day the earth suddenly brought forth forests—marvelous varieties of beasts and flocks of every kind untended on the grass—a wondrous thing to behold. Then finally the lion woke for battle; then the dread tiger and the scaly serpent; and the lioness of tawny neck grew fierce and the giant wolves howled. Other herds grazed on green herbs; flocks lacked neither clear waters nor pastures.[127]

SUGGESTED READINGS	SUGGESTED OCCASIONS
Gen 1:11–13, 20–23	Social justice days (environment)
Gen 1:24–31	Holy Week (creation account)
	Ordinary time

Proba

(Themes—Penance, Environment)

Pay attention to what I am about to say. There is in sight a tree with glorious branches, which it is forbidden to all to lay low with fire or tool. Divine law decrees that it never be disturbed. Whoever shall pluck the sacred fruit from this holy tree shall die deservedly. I shall not change my mind. Let no advisor seem so wise as to persuade you to soil your hands—my voice should be a warning to you—and let no one's force prevail over you if the glory of this divine land is to remain worthy of you.

But behold, hard upon the rising sun's first light they came to a place where soft marjoram embraced them with blossoms and sweet shade. Here is rosy spring, and summer in other months. Here clear fountains, here honey swells in seasons appointed by heaven. Here white poplar shades a cave and gentle vines weave round shady nooks. Gardens redolent with crocuses invite them in amidst groves perfumed by laurels, and the earth itself brought forth all things gladly and freely.

Now the dreadful day was at hand; behold through the flowery fields the enemy—a snake, atrocious, with immense coils, seven huge spirals, seven folds writhing—not an easy thing to look at nor easy for anyone to describe—with bitter envy it hung from a leafy bough, panting its viperous breath, its heart set on wrath, treachery and heinous crimes. Even God despised it.[128]

SUGGESTED READINGS	SUGGESTED OCCASIONS
Gen 2:8–17	Communal penance
Gen 3:1–8	Ordinary time
	Holy Week
	(creation account)

Proba

(Themes—Suffering, Hope)

From that time when people first entrusted themselves to the sea and comrades pulled ships to the tranquil deep; one with exquisite skill lashes broad waters with casting net seeking the depths while another trolls the sea with damp line. After their ships gained the deep and lands were no longer visible, the heavens lighted constantly with fiery flashes; suddenly clouds carried off the sky and the day; the winds arose and raised waves toward the stars. The comrades' blood chilled and froze with sudden fear; their spirits sank and all in tears regarded the sea—in unison they cried. Hesitating between hope and fear, they knew not whether they should plan to live or suffer the ultimate. They were within a hair's breadth of death, but such are the perils people suffer on the high seas.

But lo! God knew that the sea was churning with a mighty roar and that a storm had been let loose, God whose power is supreme. Light as the wind and swifter than a lightning bolt he sought the up-turned waters and moved across the open sea and took a stand not far from the sailing ship. The naked crew recognized from afar their King, and hailed him with loud cries. After he touched the towering waves and came to calm waters, this awesome and miraculous sight was reported: the waves subsided so that to row was no longer a struggle.[129]

SUGGESTED READINGS	SUGGESTED OCCASIONS
Isa 43:1–8	Time of trial
Jonah 1:4–16	Ordinary time

Proba

(Themes—Resurrection, Renewal)

The sky darkened with a mighty roar and black night took away colors from the world....The earth quaked, wild beasts fled and mortal hearts were laid low by abject terror, nation by nation. Then suddenly the earth gave forth a groan; the sky resounded with thunder. Immediately bodiless shades, disturbed, came up from deepest hell. The earth also and the expanses of the sea bore witness; rivers stood still and the earth split open....The sun also, although it was rising...hid its radiant face with darksome haze. Companions scattered and were swallowed up by black night and, sad in heart, they wondered at the harshness of their lot....O grief and glory, O splendor of these great events!

And now day was retracing its steps to the upper air when suddenly before their eyes the tomb with its great rock where the lifeless body had been placed—neither bolts nor the guards were strong enough to keep it there—they saw the rocks torn from rocks, tight fitting joints loosened. There was a roar, the earth was shaken by the huge weight. There was terror in every heart; the very silence was horrifying. But behold from beneath the eaves the first songs of birds. Leaving the tomb He strode, glorious in His victory; He went forth in triumph, and the earth shrilled, shook with the beat of His feet.[130]

SUGGESTED READINGS	SUGGESTED OCCASIONS
Rev 11:4–13	Easter season
Rev 16:10–18	Lenten season

Ruhm

(Themes—Suffering, Service)

Blessed Ruhm proclaimed, "The king has sent a message to me that I should deny Christ and so save my life. But I have sent reply to him, saying that, if I were to deny Christ I would die, but if I do not deny Him, then I shall live. Far be it from me, my fellow women, far be it from me that I should deny Christ my God, for it is in Him that I have faith; in His name was I baptized myself and I had my daughters baptized as well; His cross do I venerate, and for His sake I and my daughters will die, just as He died for our sakes.

My gold that belongs to the earth I leave for the earth; let anyone who wants to take my gold do so; let anyone who wants to take my silver and jewelry take them. Of my own free will I leave everything behind in order to go and receive a substitute for it from my Lord. Blessed are you, my fellow women, if you listen to my words...."[131]

SUGGESTED READINGS	SUGGESTED OCCASIONS
1 John 2:20–27	Feasts of martyrs
Rev 17:7–14	Christ the King
	Social justice days
	Ruhm's feast—
	November 20

Sarah

(Themes—Penance, Renewal)

It was related of *Amma* Sarah that for thirteen years she waged warfare against the demon of fornication. She never prayed that the warfare should cease but she said, "O God, give me strength." Once the same spirit...attacked her more intently, reminding her of the vanities of the world. But she gave herself up to the fear of God and to asceticism and went up onto her little terrace to pray. Then the spirit of fornication appeared corporally to her and said, "Sarah, you have overcome me." But she said, "It is not I who have overcome you but my master, Christ."

Amma Sarah said, "If I prayed God that all should approve of my conduct, I should find myself a penitent at the door of each one, but I shall rather pray that my heart may be pure towards all." She also said, "I put out my foot to ascend the ladder, and I place death before my eyes before going up it." She also said, "It is good to give alms to those in need. Even if it is only done to please people, through it one can begin to seek to please God."[132]

SUGGESTED READINGS	SUGGESTED OCCASIONS
1 Tim 1:3–11	Times of trial
Rev 14:1–5	Renewal times
	Sarah's feast—July 13

Sibylline Oracles

(Themes—Incarnation, Mary)

A retelling of the Incarnation story (ca. AD 175):

> In the last times God changed the earth and, coming late
> as a new light, God rose from the womb of the Virgin Mary.

Coming from heaven, God put on a mortal form.
First then, Gabriel was revealed in his strong and holy
    person.
Second, the archangel also addressed the maiden in
    speech:
Receive God, Virgin, in your immaculate bosom. Thus
    speaking, he
breathed in the grace of God, to one who was always a
    maiden.
Fear and, at the same time, wonder seized her as she
    listened.
She stood trembling. Her mind fluttered
while her heart was shaken by the unfamiliar things she
    heard.
But again she rejoiced, and her heart was healed by the
    voice.
The maiden laughed and reddened her cheek,
rejoicing with joy and enchanted in heart with awe.
Courage also came over her. A word flew to her womb.
In time it was made flesh and came to life in the womb,
and was fashioned in mortal form and became a boy
by virgin birth. For this is a great wonder for humans,
but nothing is a great wonder for God.[133]

SUGGESTED READINGS	SUGGESTED OCCASIONS
Phil 2:5–11	Christmastime
Col 1:12–20	Feasts of Mary
	Ordinary time

Sibyls

(Themes—Pentecost, Baptism)

When everything comes to pass,
then you will remember me and no longer will anyone
    say that I am crazy,
I who am a prophet of the great God.
For God did not reveal to me what God had revealed
    before to my parents
but what happened first, these things my father told
    me,
and God put all of the future in my mind
so that I prophesy both future and former things
and tell them to mortals. For when the world was
    deluged
with waters, and a certain single approved man was left
floating on the waters in a house of hewn wood
with beasts, and birds, so that the world might be filled
    again,
I was God's daughter-in-law and I was of God's blood.
The first things happened to God and all of the latter
    things have been revealed,
so let all these things from my mouth be accounted
    true.[134]

SUGGESTED READINGS	SUGGESTED OCCASIONS
Jer 1:4–10	Pentecost time
Gen 7:17–23	Ordinary time

Sibyls

(Themes—Renewal, Pentecost)

Beginning from the first generation of articulate
    persons
down to the last, I will prophesy all in turn,
such things as were before, as are, and as will come
    upon
the world through impiety.
First God bids me tell truly how the world
came to be. But you, devious mortal, so that you may
    never neglect my commands,
attentively make known the most high king. It was God
    who created
the whole world saying, "Let it come to be" and it
    came to be.
For God established the earth, draping it around with
Tartarus, and gave sweet light.
God elevated heaven, and stretched out the gleaming
    sea,
and crowned the vault of heaven amply with bright-
    shining stars
and decorated the earth with plants. God mixed the sea
with rivers, pouring them in, and with the air mingled
    fragrances
and dewy clouds. God placed another species,
fish, in the seas, and gave birds to the winds;
to the woods, also, shaggy wild beasts, and creeping
serpents to the earth; and all things which now are
    seen.[135]

SUGGESTED READINGS	SUGGESTED OCCASIONS
Gen 1:1–10	New Year
Gen 1:16–25	Holy Week
	(creation account)
	Ordinary time

Syncletica

(Theme—Spirituality)

Syncletica said, "Imitate the publican and you will not be condemned with the Pharisee. Choose the meekness of Moses and you will find your heart which is a rock changed into a spring of water."

She also said, "It is dangerous for anyone to teach who has not first been trained in the 'practical' life. For someone who owns a ruined house and receives guests there does them harm because of the dilapidation of his or her dwelling. It is the same in the case of someone who has not first built an interior dwelling; that one causes loss to those who come. By words one may convert them to salvation, but by evil behavior, one injures them."[136]

SUGGESTED READINGS	SUGGESTED OCCASIONS
Heb 3:1–6	Dedication of the church
Hag 1:2–10	Pentecost season
	Ordinary time

Syncletica

(Themes—Penance, Spirituality)

Amma Syncletica said, "There is an asceticism which is determined by the enemy and his disciples practice it. So how are we to distinguish between the divine and royal asceticism and the demonic tyranny? Clearly through its quality of balance. Always use a single rule of fasting. Do not fast four or five days and break it the following day with any amount of food. In truth lack of proportion always corrupts. While you are young and healthy, fast, for old age with its weakness will come. As long as you can, lay up treasure, so that when you cannot, you will be at peace."

She also said, "There are many who live in the mountains and behave as if they were in the town, and they are wasting their time. It is possible to be a solitary in one's mind while living in a crowd, and it is possible for one who is solitary to live in the crowd of one's thoughts."[137]

SUGGESTED READINGS	SUGGESTED OCCASIONS
1 Cor 9:19–27	Lent
Rule of Benedict,	Renewal days
chapter 40	Syncletica's feast—
	January 5

Syncletica

(Themes—Penance, Stability)

Amma Syncletica said, "If you find yourself in a monastery do not go to another place, for that will harm you a great deal. Just as the bird who abandons the eggs she was sitting on prevents them from hatching, so the monk or the nun grows cold and their faith dies, when they go from one place to another."

She also said, "If illness weighs us down, let us not be sorrowful as though, because of the illness and the prostration of our bodies, we could not sing, for all these things are for our good, for the purification of our desires. Truly fasting and sleeping on the ground are set before us because of our sensuality. If illness then weakens this sensuality the reason for these practices is superfluous. For this is the great asceticism: to control oneself in illness and to sing hymns of thanksgiving to God."[138]

SUGGESTED READINGS	SUGGESTED OCCASIONS
Jas 5:13–18	Community days
Rule of Benedict,	Times of trial
chapter 1.6–11	Syncletica's feast—
	January 5

Teresa of Avila

(Theme—Prayer)

Not long ago a very learned person told me that souls who do not practice prayer are like people with paralyzed or crippled bodies; even though they have hands and feet they cannot give orders to these hands and feet. Thus there are souls so ill and so accustomed to being involved in external matters that there is no remedy, nor does it seem they can enter within themselves. They are so used to dealing with the insects and vermin that are in the wall surrounding the castle that they have become almost like them. And though they have a rich nature and the power to converse with none other than God, there is no remedy. If these souls do not strive to understand and cure their great misery, they will be changed into statues of salt, unable to turn their heads to look at themselves, just as Lot's wife was changed for having turned her head.

Insofar as I can understand, the gate of entry to the castle is prayer and reflection. I don't mean to refer to mental more than vocal prayer, for since vocal prayer is prayer it must be accompanied by reflection. A prayer in which a person is not aware to whom they are speaking, what they are asking, who it is who is asking and of whom, I do not call prayer however much the lips may move....Anyone who has the habit of speaking before God's majesty as though they were speaking to a slave or saying whatever comes into their head, in my opinion is not praying. Please God, may no Christians pray in this way.[139]

SUGGESTED READINGS	SUGGESTED OCCASIONS
Gen 19:12–26	Prayer days
Rom 8:18–27	Advent
1 Cor 2:6–16	Ordinary time
	Teresa's feast—
	October 15

Teresa of Avila

(Themes—Humility, Discernment)

Humility, like the bee making honey in the beehive, is always at work. Without it, everything goes wrong. But let us remember that the bee doesn't fail to leave the beehive and fly about gathering nectar from the flowers. So it is with the soul in the room of self-knowledge; let it fly sometimes to ponder the grandeur and majesty of its God. Here it will discover its lowliness better than by thinking of itself, and be freer from the vermin that enter the first rooms, those of self-knowledge. It is by the mercy of God that a person practices self-knowledge. Believe me, we shall practice much better virtue through God's help than by being tied down to our own misery.

I don't know if this has been explained well. Knowing ourselves is something so important that I wouldn't want any relaxation ever in this regard, however high you may have climbed into the heavens. While we are on this earth nothing is more important to us than humility. So I repeat that it is good, indeed very good, to try to enter first into the room where self-knowledge is dealt with rather than to fly off to other rooms. This is the right road, and if we can journey along a safe and level path, why should we want wings to fly? So let us strive to make more progress in self-knowledge, for in my opinion we shall never completely know ourselves if we don't strive to know God. Gazing at God's grandeur, we get in touch with our own lowliness; by looking at God's purity, we shall see our own filth; and by pondering God's humility, we shall see how far we are from being humble.[140]

SUGGESTED READINGS	SUGGESTED OCCASIONS
Col 3:1–4, 12–17	Advent
1 Pet 5:1–11	Renewal days
Eph 3:14–4:6	Prayer days
Rule of Benedict,	Teresa's feast—
chapter 7.5–13	October 15

Teresa of Avila

(Themes—Love, Service)

I sometimes remember the complaint of that holy woman, Martha. Her complaint was not merely of her sister—I feel sure that the chief cause of her sorrow was the thought that you, Lord, had no compassion on her for the labor that she was enduring nor cared whether or not she was with you. Perhaps she thought that you had less love for her than for her sister, and this would have troubled her more than serving the One whom she loved so dearly, for love turns labor into rest.

And so she said nothing to her sister, but made her complaint to You alone, for love made her bold enough to ask why You had no care for her. Your answer seems to imply that the source of her complaint was that it is love alone which gives value to all things and that the most needful thing is that it should be so great that nothing can hinder its operation.[141]

SUGGESTED READINGS	SUGGESTED OCCASIONS
Deut 7:6–11	Martha's feast—July 29
Song 8:4–7	Prayer days
	Teresa's feast—
	October 15

Teresa of Avila

(Theme—Prayer)

Let us not consider how this garden [of prayer] can be watered, so that we may know what we have to do, what labor it will cost us, if the gain will outweigh the labor and for how long this labor must be borne. It seems to me that the garden can be watered in four ways: by taking water from a well, which costs us great labor; or by a water-wheel and buckets, when the water is drawn by a windlass (I have sometimes drawn it in this way; it is less laborious than the other and gives more water). Or it can be watered by a stream or a brook, which waters the ground much better, for it saturates it more thoroughly and there is less need to water it often, lessening the gardener's labor. Finally, there can be heavy rain, when the Lord waters the garden with no labor of ours, a way incomparably better than any of those which have been described.[142]

SUGGESTED READINGS　　**SUGGESTED OCCASIONS**

Jas 5:7–8, 13–18　　Prayer days

2 Chr 6:14–21　　Teresa's feast—

October 15

Ordinary time

Teresa of Avila

(Theme—Spirituality)

When the Lord begins to implant a virtue in us, it must be esteemed very highly and we must on no account run the risk of losing it. So it is in matters concerning our reputation and in many others. You can be quite sure that we are not all completely detached when we think we are and it is essential that we should never be careless about this. If anyone wishing to make progress in spiritual matters finds that they are becoming fussy about their reputation, let them believe what I say and put this attachment right behind them, for it is a chain which no file can sever: only God can break it, with the aid of prayer and great effort on our part.[143]

SUGGESTED READINGS	SUGGESTED OCCASIONS
1 Cor 3:16–23	Renewal days
Eph 4:17–24	Penitential time
	Lent
	Teresa's feast—
	October 15

Teresa of Avila

(Themes—Suffering, Spirituality)

We always find that those who walk closest to Christ our Lord were those who had to bear the greatest trials. Consider the trials suffered by his glorious Mother and the Apostles. How do you suppose Saint Paul could endure such terrible trials? We can see in his life the effects of genuine visions and contemplation coming from our Lord and not from human imagination or from the deceit of the devil. Do you imagine that he shut himself up with his visions so as to enjoy those Divine favors and pursue no other occupation? You know very well that…he took not a day's rest, nor can he have rested by night, since it was then that he had to earn his living.

I am very fond of the story of how, when Saint Peter was fleeing from prison, our Lord appeared to him and told him to go back to Rome and be crucified. We never recite the Office on his feast, in which this story is found, without my deriving a special consolation from it. How did Saint Peter feel after receiving this favor? And what did he do? He went straight to his death; and the Lord showed him no small mercy in providing someone to kill him.[144]

SUGGESTED READINGS	SUGGESTED OCCASIONS
2 Cor 12:1–10	Lent
Acts 23:6–11	Times of trial
	Teresa's feast—
	October 15

Theodora

(Themes—Prayer, Spirituality)

Amma Theodora said, "It is good to live in peace, for the wise person practices perpetual prayer. It is truly a great thing for a virgin or a monk to live in peace, especially for the younger ones. However, you should realize that as soon as you intend to live in peace, at once evil comes and weighs down your soul through *accidie*, faintheartedness, and evil thoughts. It also attacks your body through sickness, debility, weakening of the knees, and all the members. It dissipates the strength of soul and body, so that one believes one is ill and no longer able to pray. But if we are vigilant, all these temptations fall away. There was, in fact, a nun who was seized by cold and fever every time she began to pray, and she suffered from headaches, too. In this condition, she said to herself 'I am ill, and near to death; so now I will get up before I die and pray.' Reasoning in this way, she did violence to herself and prayed. When she had finished, the fever abated also. So, by reasoning in this way, the sister resisted, and prayed and was able to conquer her thoughts."[145]

SUGGESTED READINGS	SUGGESTED OCCASIONS
Isa 55:3–9	Prayer days
Rom 14:12–19	Ordinary time
	Theodora's feast—
	September 1

Theodora

(Themes—Humility, Spirituality)

Amma Theodora said that a teacher ought to be a stranger to the desire for domination, vain-glory, and pride; one should not be able to fool her by flattery, nor blind her by gifts, nor conquer her by the stomach, nor dominate her by anger; but she should be patient, gentle and humble as far as possible; she must be tested and without partisanship, full of concern, and a lover of souls.

The same *amma* was asked about the conversations one hears. "If one is habitually listening to worldly speech, how can one yet live for God alone, as you suggest?" She said, "Just as when you are sitting at table and there are many courses, you take some but without pleasure, so when worldly conversations come your way, have your heart turned towards God. Thanks to this disposition, you will hear them without pleasure, and they will not do you any harm."[146]

SUGGESTED READINGS	SUGGESTED OCCASIONS
Phil 2:1–6	Prayer days
Jer 48:25–33	Theodora's feast—
	September 1
	Ordinary time

Marie de France

(Themes—Service, Stewardship)

Fable of the Dog and the Ewe...

This tells of a lying dog
with nasty tricks, a deceiver,
who brought suit against a ewe.
He took her to court,
claiming some bread
which he had, so he said, lent her.
The ewe denied it all
and said he had lent her nothing.
The judge asked the dog
whether he had any witnesses.
He answered he had two,
the kite and the wolf.
They were brought forth
and affirmed, by oath,
that what the dog said was true.
Do you know why they did it?
Because they expected a share
if the ewe lost her life.
The judge then asked
the ewe, whom he cited,
why she had denied the bread
which the dog had given her.
She had lied for a small amount,
now let her pay before it got worse.
The poor thing didn't have enough
so she had to sell her wool.
It was winter and she died of the cold.
The dog came and took her wool.
and the kite as well,
and then the wolf, but it was too late,

for the meat had been torn up by them,
since they were in need of food.
And the ewe did not live—
her lord lost her completely.
This example should show us:
it can be proven of many
that by lying and deceit
they frequently bring the poor to court;
they often find false witnesses
whom they pay with the belongings of the poor.
They don't care what becomes of the victims
as long as each of them gets his share.[147]

SUGGESTED READINGS	**SUGGESTED OCCASIONS**
2 Sam 12:1–10	Lent
Jas 2:1–8	Social justice days
	Communal penance

Biographical
Sketches

Aemiliana Löhr—Aemiliana was born in Dusseldorf, Germany (1896–1972), and died in the Benedictine monastery of Herstelle, also in Germany. She is the most contemporary writer in this collection. She studied literature and philosophy at the University of Cologne before she entered the monastery in 1927. Aemiliana was chronicler for her community for years, but spent most of her time writing. Familiar with the works of Pius Parsch and Odo Casel, popular liturgical writers at the time, her own works, for example, *The Mother of Salvation and The Great Week*, also deal with liturgical subjects.

Anahid[1]—Anahid was a Persian martyr of the fifth century. She became a Christian after she had been healed, twice—once when she was possessed by an evil spirit and later when she had leprosy. Her father, who had sent her to be healed by the Christian, Pethion, was at first angered by her conversion but eventually was converted himself after being healed by the holy man. Anahid was hidden by other Christians for a time, but eventually the authorities caught up with her. She is said to have greeted them with, "What do you want, sirs? If it is me you are looking for, here I am, a sinful lamb ready to be sacrificed. Have no fear, I will go with you gladly." After many tortures, including sexual mutilation, she was finally stretched out on the ground and smeared with honey and left to the elements, held there by four huge iron stakes. The account says that an enormous swarm of wasps collected over her like a cloud, preventing anyone from coming near her. Finally, when some of the clergy came to pray there, they found her praying and commending her spirit to God. The account of Anahid is typical of many women-martyrs at this time in history. The storyteller seems to want to show that evil things are done by evil people and that nature refuses to participate in such activity.

Angela Merici—Angela (1474–1540) spent her early years in the lake country of Lombardy, Italy. A prayerful child, she once had a vision in which she saw her sister Eletta, her childhood companion who died at an early age. Eletta was smiling and told her that she would found a "company of virgins" in Brescia before she died. Later, Angela spent much time helping the poor of Brescia and often gathered young girls around her, teaching them Christian doctrine. These practices eventually led her to found the Ursulines, the group predicted by her sister. Her feast is January 27.

Birgitta of Sweden—Birgitta, a cousin of King Magnus of Sweden, was born (1302 or 1303) on her father's estate about fifty miles north of Stockholm. Her pious parents carefully raised their children in the faith. When Birgitta was seven years old, she received her first vision. At age thirteen, she was betrothed to a young nobleman. They married and had eight children. After her husband died, she had a conversion experience that persuaded her to give her whole being to Christ as his bride. All her life she had revelations, but after this they became more numerous. She founded the religious Order of the Most Holy Savior (a double community of both nuns and priests), and had great influence on leaders, both religious and civil, in the Europe of her day. She was canonized by Pope Boniface IX in 1391, only eighteen years after her death. Her feast is July 23.

Blandina—The only information we have on Blandina is found in the *Ecclesiastical History* written by the fourth-century church historian Eusebius. The passage that mentions her in his account describes the death of a group of martyrs under the ruler Marcus Aurelius in Gaul during the summer of AD 177. She, a slave woman arrested with her mistress, was the most heroic of them all. Under torture she said repeatedly, "I am a Christian and nothing wicked happens among us." When she was tied to the stake, the wild beasts did not touch her. The pagans who were present said they never saw a woman suffer so long and so much. Her feast is June 2.

Brigit of Kildare—Brigit, who lived in Ireland from about 452 to 524 is the most famous female leader of the early Celtic Church. She governed both women and men in her double monastery at Kildare and was considered a spiritual guide par excellence. She was called the "Mary of the Gael" and, during the Middle Ages, she was considered the patron saint of travelers and pilgrims. In Ireland, she is still prayed to as the guardian of farm animals, of healers, and of midwives. Her feast is February 1.

Catherine of Genoa—Catherine (1447–1510) was born into an aristocratic family and married into another one. Ten years after her marriage she had a profound religious experience. Her husband, after a life of infidelity, experienced a religious conversion also and, together, they began working at the Pammatone Hospital that served the sick poor in Genoa. Catherine remained there until her death, serving as its director from 1490 to 1496. Her life was marked by personal penance and remarkable mystical experiences. The works attributed to her, *Purgation and Purgatory* and *The Spiritual Dialogue*, actually were not written by her personally. Rather, these writings are her teachings, later recounted by her friends and then written down. Her feast is September 14.

Catherine of Siena—Catherine was born in Siena in 1347, the twenty-fourth child of twenty-five. Her confessor and life-long friend, Raymond of Capua, is her biographer. One of his stories records a vision she had at age six of Jesus, which prompted her to vow her virginity to God the next year. To follow through on this promise, she cut off her hair when her relatives tried to make her more attractive at the marriageable age of fifteen. Catherine lived in an age of stark contrasts. It was a century of such great mystics as Meister Eckhart, John Tauler, and Julian of Norwich, and it was the dark age of the church known as the "Avignon Papacy" when the pope lived in luxury in France rather than in Rome. Catherine, a liberated woman, admonished Pope Gregory XI to reform his clergy, and urged him to take part in the Crusades and to return to Rome. A spiritual encounter Catherine had after he returned led her to write her famous work, *The Dialogue*. She died on Ascension Thursday, April 29, 1380 (now her feast). Pope Paul VI declared her a doctor of the church on October 4, 1970.

Dhuoda—Dhuoda (ca. 803–843) lived in southern France at the time of the breakup of the Carolingian Empire. Her book, the *Manual*, is a kind of moral guide, written in the form of a letter to her son, William. From it we learn how well-read she was in scripture, in the fathers of the church, and in the Christian poets of the ninth century as well as how, from a woman's point of view, she saw this turbulent time in history. Her motherly concern for her son at the time is evident as well as some of the more intimate details of her home life. Much of her writing includes exhortations for her son, urging him to practice the Christian virtues of justice and courage, protection of widows and orphans, charity to the poor, and practicing reverence for those who exercised authority in the church and in civil society.

Egeria—Egeria of Spain (fl.c. 381–384), was a Christian woman who, after the persecutions of Christians had ended with the Council of Nicea in AD 325, followed the suggestion of Constantine that people once again visit the holy places of the Middle East. A wealthy person, she traveled from north-west Spain to Asia Minor, Palestine, and Egypt. She left a detailed record, in Latin, of her three-year journey. This record is important for us in that it gives us a clear picture of what some of the earliest liturgical practices were in the church, some of them strikingly similar to our own, especially those during Holy Week.

Elizabeth[1]—Elizabeth, another one of the "Holy Women of the Syrian Orient," was a deaconess and a leader of the perse-cuted church of the Arabian peninsula. From a house where Christians had been hiding her, she rushed to enter a burning church where the bones of her brother, a former bishop, were buried. The Jews thought she was escaping and seized her. Elizabeth told them, on the contrary, "I want to be burnt in the church where I have ministered, together with my brother's bones." The account reports that she was forty-seven years old at the time. The bones of her body were stretched violently and her head burned with boiling oil. A clay crown was placed on her head, and she was told, "Receive your crown, servant of the carpenter's son!" Finally, she was stripped naked and tied to a wild camel that jerked her along violently into the desert until she died. She was buried by two male relatives who risked their lives to honor her memory.

Eudokia—The earliest information we have about Eudokia indicates that she was born at the beginning of the fifth cen-tury and that she was the daughter of the pagan philosopher Leontios, who named her "Athenais," after the place of her birth, Athens. No reason is given for her leaving Athens to go to Constantinople, but it was there she fell in love with and married a young Byzantine ruler. By this time she had converted to Christianity and took the name "Eudokia," which means "good will" or "good pleasure." She received the additional name, "Augusta," from the emperor as a sign of respect and honor. Much of the rest of her life was given over to writing and the patronage of churches, monasteries, and other charities. On June 14, 460, she was at the consecration of the Church of St. Stephen outside of Jerusalem, and on October 20 of the same year she died and was buried there.

Gertrude of Helfta—Most authors agree that Gertrude (also spelled "Gertrud") was born January 5, 1256, but the date of her death has been placed between 1301 and 1303. Other than this, the first durable historical fact we have about her is that she was confided to the nuns at the Helfta in Germany at the age of five. Here she was raised and educated in Latin, philosophy, and theology. Another famous Gertrude (of Hackeborn) was abbess of the monastery and the young Gertrude was entrusted to the abbess's sister, St. Mechtild, who soon became her soul-friend. Gertrude had her first visionary experience at age twenty-five or twenty-six. Jesus showed himself to her as a young boy of about sixteen. He reproached her for being so caught up in her studies that her prayer was hindered. From then on she practiced a continual remembrance of the presence of God that she never lost. Because of her holiness and ability to discern spirits, the abbess encouraged her nuns to seek Gertrude's advice. She was reluctant to speak of the favors she had received from the Lord, but Jesus told St. Mechtild there was no dwelling place so pleasing to him as the heart of Gertrude. The Sacred Heart devotion, promulgated later with St. Margaret Mary Alacoque, had its beginnings with St. Gertrude, when Jesus said, "I give you my Heart...that it may supply all your incapacities." Her feast is November 16.

Hadewijch[2]—Hadewijch was a Flemish Beguine of the thirteenth century. Biographical information about her is very scanty except for the fact that she was a Beguine, belonging to the women's movement of her day. One story claims that on a Sunday after Pentecost, Hadewijch felt unable to go to the church for Eucharist. A priest unobtrusively brought her communion and after receiving the sacrament she was drawn into deep union with Christ. She found herself in a vast meadow where an angel guided her to an understanding of the symbolism of the trees growing there. Of one tree he said, "You climb this tree from beginning to end, all the way to the profound roots of the incomprehensible God!" Hadewijch understood this climbing of the tree as arriving at the knowledge of God through an ascent of faith and hope, nearest to us, and charity, which is nearest to God. She passed on what she learned from her visions to the contemplative group that she headed. Her life, experiences, and writings, after passing through the hands of John of Ruusbroec (1293–1318), were lost for centuries. No "life" of Hadewijch was ever printed. It is only today that her writings have once again been made available to us.

Hild of Whitby—Hild, an Anglo-Saxon abbess, was born in Northumbria in 614. She founded a number of monasteries in northern England, including the double monastery at Whitby. The monastic school there became famous for its fine education. At least five of its students became bishops and her protégé Caedmon was the first English poet. She died in 680 of a lengthy and painful illness, probably tuberculosis. Her feast is November 17.

Hildegard of Bingen—Hildegard (1098–1179), a Benedictine nun and mystic, was born into a noble family in the Rhineland. When she was only five years old, she had her first vision of light. Three years later, her parents placed her in the convent at Disibodenberg where she was tutored by the anchoress Jutta, eventually succeeding her as head of the community in 1136. Five years later, she experienced a vision of great radiance in which a heavenly voice commanded her to write about what she saw. Reluctantly, she recorded the visions she had over the next ten years. The resulting book, *Scivias* ("Know Thy Ways"), was only one of Hildegard's accomplishments. She produced works of drama, music, mysticism, prophecy, cosmology, the lore of animals and gems, medicine, and three other books of allegorical visions. She corresponded with rulers and popes and was famous for her travels and the preaching she did throughout the towns and cities of Germany. These merited for her the title, "Sibyl of the Rhine." Her feast is September 17.

Jane de Chantal—Jane Frances de Chantal never knew her mother who died in childbirth when Jane was eighteen months old. She and her older sister, and the brother who survived this birth, were raised by their father, a lawyer in Dijon, France. When she was twenty, she married Baron Christophe de Cantalman. They had six children, four of whom survived infancy. Two weeks after the last child was born, her beloved husband was killed in a freak hunting accident. Several years later, Jane went with her father to hear a series of Lenten sermons given by Francis de Sales. She had been struggling with grief over her husband's death, while at the same time she began to sense within herself a new hungering for God. Francis de Sales became her director and a lasting friend. Together, they discerned her spiritual aspirations. This led to the cofounding, in 1610, of a women's congregation, the Visitation of Holy Mary. Most of the writings we have from Jane's pen are letters she wrote to members of this community. Her feast is August 18.

Julian of Norwich—Julian (1343–1416/1419), was an English anchoress. She was probably born in Yorkshire. Her parentage is unknown, though she does speak of her mother being at her bedside at a time when it was thought she was dying. Some surmise she must have had a happy childhood since she shows such a natural and spontaneous delight in God. Later, at a date not known, she lived as a recluse with one servant, in a cell attached to the church wall of St. Julian in Conisford at Norwich. She took its name for her own. Norwich was an important city in the fourteenth century. Across the lane from her anchorhold was a house of Augustinian friars. From this information, it is believed she had ample opportunity for learning. She could have received further training from a tutor or the nuns at the Benedictine priory of Carrow. Though her most famous work, *Showings*, was almost forgotten until the seventeenth century, today there is much more interest in her writing. She is best known for her teachings on the Motherhood of God. Her feast is May 8.

Leoba—Leoba (also spelled "Lioba") was an eighth-century Anglo-Saxon nun. As a young girl, she was sent to a woman's monastery for her education. There she was noted for her moderation, common sense, charity, and love of learning. Her tutor, the famous abbess Tetta, governed monasteries of both women and men. Leoba became so famous in her monastery that St. Boniface asked her to accompany him as his partner in his missionary work to the people of Germany. She proved to be a wise monastic superior. She was asked to counsel both rulers and bishops. Her feast is September 28.

Margery Kempe—Margery was born around 1373 in Lynn, which was then one of the major trade centers of England. Around 1393 she married John Kempe, a prominent businessman of Lynn. *The Book of Margery Kempe* is a kind of auto-biography, though undoubtedly written by someone else at her dictation since she, like other nonclerical contemporaries, was probably unable to read or write. She was the mother of fourteen children. The birth of her first child was so stressful for her that she went through what spiritual writers term, "the dark night of the soul." After that her life changed and she had visions and revelations from then on. She made many journeys and pilgrimages and it seems that she was acquainted with Julian of Norwich. Her husband died in 1431 and the last mention we have of her is in 1438 when the second part of her writing was being completed. The date of her death is not recorded.

Marguerite Porete[2]—Marguerite, like her contemporary Mechtild of Magdeburg, was a Beguine. Unlike Mechtild, however, her writings have remained relatively unknown. She is, perhaps, the most neglected of the great writers of the thirteenth century. This is because the language she used to describe her experience of divine love seemed provocative and deliberately shocking to the clergy of her day who tried to suppress her works. She wrote her *Mirror of Simple Souls*, a book of poetic prose, dialogue, and lyrics sometime between 1285 and 1295. Her works were condemned around 1300 but this did not shake her convictions or cause her to renounce them. She was imprisoned, tried, and executed by being publicly burned in Paris on June 1, 1310. Though vigorous attempts were made to do away with all her work, her *Mirror* was preserved by those who cherished these writings. Her feast is June 1.

Martha[1]—Martha, one of the "Holy Women of the Syrian Orient," lived in the middle of the fourth century in what is now Iraq and western Iran. Syrian Christians and Greek-

speaking Christians who were prisoners of war were perse-
cuted by the Zoroastrian authorities. These authorities were
as much angered by Martha's vow of virginity as by her faith
since such a vow was abhorrent to their mores. Young women
who took this vow were known as "daughters of the
covenant." Martha was martyred with three other of these
"daughters." Their torturer demanded, "Do the king's will;
worship the sun, and get married. If you do this, you will avoid
beating, and you will save yourself from the sentence of death
by the sword." After a beating, they said, "We will not
exchange God for the sun; we will not become foolish and
senseless like you who have abandoned the Creator and wor-
shipped instead what God has created." Then they were
beheaded. According to the account, Martha was martyred
while saying prayers with strong eucharistic overtones.

Mechtild of Magdeburg[2]—Mechtild (ca. 1207–1282/1294),
like Hildegard of Bingen, was a German mystic who wrote
down her experiences. She began to write *The Flowing Light of
the Godhead* when she was forty-three, though her first "greeting" from the Holy Spirit occurred when she was twelve years
old. The seven books of this prophetic work represent the different stages of her experience. From this work, we also glean
something about her life. She was born in the diocese of
Magdeburg to a well-to-do family. She left home when she was
twenty-three and joined the Beguines. Twelve years before her
death, she entered the Benedictine community at Helfta in
Saxony. In thirteenth-century England all the writings on mysticism were written by men, but on the continent they were
written by nuns. For this reason, Helfta was unique because it
was the center of such writings. Her feast is November 19.

Olympias—Olympias (ca. 365–410) was a wealthy noblewoman of the capital city of Constantinople who joined

monastic life in the middle of the city rather than in the usual desert regions. She became a widow early in life and refused a second marriage so she could follow Christ in the ascetic life. Olympias donated most of her property to the poor and to the church. She was ordained a deaconess by her friend John Chrysostom. When he was exiled, she remained loyal to him despite both civil and ecclesiastical pressure and so she, too, was exiled. After her death, miraculous appearances indicated how and where she was to be buried. Soon a popular devotion to her arose as well as reports of multiple healings. Her feast is December 16.

Perpetua—Everything we know about Perpetua is given in a third-century document that records her martyrdom. It is unique in that it is the first account of Christian protest that we have and because much of the information in it was gathered from women. Unlike other documents from the third century which contain embellishments, this is a first-hand account. It is also important for us because it shows us the value system of the early Christians who, through their suffering and death, gave witness to freedom and truth. Though history at this time rarely recorded the accomplishments of women, martyrdom raised them up as equals with men in the struggle for liberation and self-fulfillment. The account speaks for itself as far as Perpetua's personality and character are concerned. She, her slave-girl, Felicitas, and five other friends were arrested in Carthage during the persecution by Septimius Severus in 202 to 203. Her feast is March 7.

Proba—Proba's name is found in the twelfth line of the work, *Cento*, which is attributed to her. The few records we have of her life indicate that she was a Roman matron whose family, the Anicii, was distinguished by members who held consulates and prefectures who exercised much power through their offices. Proba's character was respectable, dignified, and some sources specify, generous. She may have been a convert to Christianity in midlife and then lived as a lay person in the lifestyle common to a woman of the Roman privileged class, that is, one of great leisure. She spent her time studying the classical writers, especially Virgil. The dates of her birth and death are not available, but the date given for her work, *Cento*, is 351, which would place her life span in the middle of the fourth century.

Ruhm[1]—Ruhm, one of the "Holy Women of the Syrian Orient," was a Syrian martyr of the sixth century. Three days after some freeborn women had gone to their deaths, Ruhm, who had been spared temporarily because of her high standing as a noblewoman, stripped off the veil women were obliged to wear and ran out into the streets condemning their persecutors and encouraging the Christians to remain steadfast. She told the women of Najran, "Gaze on me, for you have seen my face only two times—at my first wedding feast, and at this, my second one." Then, telling them the king had sent a message to her to deny Christ and save herself, she said her reply to the king was, "…if I were to deny Christ I would die, but if I do not deny Him, then I shall live." After that, the account reads, she was tortured first by having her granddaughter and one of her daughters executed before her eyes and having their blood poured into her mouth. When asked how her daughter's blood tasted she replied, "Like a pure, spotless offering…." Enraged, the king had her beheaded. The date given for these martyrs is November 20, also considered their feast.

Sarah[3]—*Amma* Sarah was recognized for her outstanding qualities of virtue and leadership among many famous figures of the early monastic movement during the fifth century. It is related that some monks of Scetis came one day to visit her and she offered them a small basket of fruit. When they left the good fruit and ate the bad, she said to them, "You are true monks of Scetis." Some of her sayings indicate that she did not hesitate to prove her virility to men who tried to ridicule her as a "mere" woman. Her feast is July 13.

Sibylline Oracles—These writings are attributed to female seers or prophets known as "sibyls." Strictly speaking, they cannot be classified as "Church Mothers" for their oracles were Jewish writings. They are important for us, however, because they were later adapted by Christian prophets. In the readings here, a sibyl retells the incarnation story (ca. AD 175).

Syncletica[3]—*Amma* Syncletica was a wise monastic woman in the fifth-century Egyptian desert. Her sayings, many of them aphorisms, were preserved by her disciples. Many of the images she uses are practical, and her asceticism stresses the need for balance. Because various of her sayings are nautical images, it is supposed by some that she grew up near the seaport of Alexandria. It is interesting to find there is no distinction made between the writings and sayings of the desert Mothers (*ammas*) and those of the desert Fathers. They are included with them. Her feast is January 5.

Teresa of Avila—Teresa, often called "the great" to distinguish her from the "little flower," was, together with her spiritual director St. John of the Cross, famous for her mystical experiences and for the reformation of the Carmelites in the sixteenth century. She was born on March 28, 1515, and died on October 4, 1582. As a child, she was so determined to be a martyr at the hand of the Moors of Africa and to bring all people to God, that she persuaded her favorite brother who was only eleven to run away with her. Fortunately, their uncle saw them and intercepted these plans. A prolific writer and a tireless worker in her efforts to reform the Carmelites, she founded many monasteries and traveled extensively via crude means of transportation. She paved the way for a better understanding of the mystical life through her classics, *The Way of Perfection* and the *Interior Castle*. In her autobiography, the *Life*, we come to know, as well, a person who, on a daily basis, lived a practical, yet intimate relationship with Jesus. She preceded Catherine of Siena in being honored with the title, doctor of the church. Her feast is October 15.

Theodora[3]—*Amma* Theodora was a famous ascetic of the fifth-century Egyptian desert. Palladius mentions a Theodora, "the wife of the tribune who reached such a depth of poverty that she became a recipient of alms and finally died in the monastery of Hesychas near the sea." She consulted Archbishop Theophilus and appears to be a woman consulted by many monks about monastic life. Many of her sayings show her wisdom about illness and temptation. Some of her teachings also stress the value of humility. Her feast is September 1.

Marie de France—Marie was a nobly born woman, originally from France, who lived and wrote in England during the last half of the twelfth century. Since she only identifies herself as "Marie," her exact identity is not certain. Some have suggested that she was the daughter of Eleanor of Aquitaine or perhaps the abbess of Shaftesbury. What is certain is that she was the first of the great, well-educated French women writers. She wrote during the period known as a time of a renaissance of thought and learning and a growing sense of the individual. To sign her name on her own work was an indication of this latter tendency. Marie wrote her love stories from a female point of view. She rejected the more popular forms of writing that glorified war and manly valor.

1. Holy Women of the Syrian Orient were Persian and Syrian women, many of them martyrs under a purge by Zoroastrian authorities. Their lives were based on eyewitness accounts, but it is evident that these were embellished at times to teach a lesson. The crimes for which they were killed were largely related to the "ceremony of consecrating the bread." Considering the times in which these women lived and the societal restraints imposed on them, their actions show how little they fit the pious mold that was supposed to be theirs. Their extraordinary feats of courage were accomplished, not by their choice to break out of the restrictions of their day but, rather, because they were compelled do so by that which is beyond themselves, that is, the conviction that it was God who called them to action. Their accounts give an excellent picture of the religious struggles from the fourth to seventh centuries in the Syrian Orient. Written originally in the Syriac language, they were not translated and edited until 1887. This was done with the intention of showing how valuable the lives of these women were to the larger church.

2. The Beguines comprised a sisterhood movement that flourished in France, Germany, Belgium, and the Netherlands around the thirteenth and fourteenth centuries. The Beguines did not follow a specific rule, did not profess vows, and did not always live a community life. They were simply women who chose to live a contemplative life in poverty, supporting themselves by the labor of their hands.

3. The *ammas* were wise women ascetics who usually lived in the desert. At the dawn of the Christian era women helped in

the Christianization of the world in such leadership roles (indicated on ancient tombstones) as rulers of the synagogue, deaconesses, presbyters, and "honorable women-bishops." However, when Christianity became the official religion in the fourth century, societal customs began relegating them to their homes. While some church officials continued offering women roles of preaching, teaching, and living as ascetics, others did not. Women strongly desiring to follow Christ began to live monastic lives in their homes and then later moved to the marginalized regions of the desert. Some lived alone; others had companions. Some of these women were recognized as having special prophetic vision and were sought out for guidance in living out their monastic life. These "spiritual elders" were the *ammas*.

Further Readings

Allchin, A.M., and Esther de Waal, *Threshold of Light: Prayers and Praises from the Celtic Tradition*, Springfield IL: Templegate, 1988.

Axters, Stephanus, OP, *The Spirituality of the Old Low Countries*, translated by Donald Attwater, London: Blackfriars, 1954, pp. 9–40; 84–85.

Bouyer, Louis, *Introduction to Spirituality*, translated by Mary Perkins Ryan, Collegeville, MN: Liturgical Press, 1961.

Brock, Sebastian, and Susan Ashbrook Harvey, translators, *Holy Women of the Syrian Orient*, Berkeley: University of California Press, 1987.

Bynum, Caroline Walker, *Jesus as Mother: Studies in the Spirituality of the High Middle Ages*, Berkeley: University of California Press, 1982.

Chadwick, Nora, *The Age of the Saints in the Early Celtic Church*, London: Oxford University Press, 1961.

Clark, Elizabeth A., *Women in the Early Church*, Message of the Fathers of the Church, Collegeville, MN: Liturgical Press, 1990.

Collis, Louise, *Memoirs of a Medieval Woman: The Life and Times of Margery Kempe*, 1964, New York: Colophon-Harper, 1983.

Conlan, Sister Mary Samuel, OP, "Bridget of Sweden, St.," vol. 2, p. 799, *New Catholic Encyclopedia*, 15 vols., New York: McGraw, 1967.

Corcopino, Joseph, *Daily Life in Ancient Rome*, New Haven: Yale University Press, 1940.

Duckett, Eleanor Shipley, "Dhuoda and Bernard of Septimania," taken from *Medieval Portraits from East and West*, pp. 197–218, Ann Arbor MI: University of Michigan Press, 1972.

Gertrude the Great of Helfta, *Spiritual Exercises*, translated by G. Jaron and J. Lewis, Kalamazoo, MI: Cistercian Publications, 1989 (CF 49).

Gingras, George E., translator, *Egeria: Diary of a Pilgrimage*. Ancient Christian Writers, New York: Newman Press, 1970.

Hughes, Kathleen, and Ann Hamlin, *Celtic Monasticism*, New York: Seabury Press, 1981.

Martin, Mary Lou, translated with text, *The Fables of Marie de France*, Birmingham, AL: Summa Publications, 1984.

Penrose, Sister Mary E., OSB, *Roots Deep and Strong: Great Men and Women of the Church*, Mahwah, NJ: Paulist Press, 1995.

Perrin, Joseph Marie, *Catherine of Siena*, translated by Paul Barrett, Westminster, MD: Neman Press, 1965.

Reuther, Rosemary Radford, "Mothers of the Church: Ascetic Women in the Late Patristic Age," in R. Ruether and E. McLaughlin, eds., *Women of Spirit: Female Leadership in the Jewish and Christian Traditions*, New York: Simon and Schuster, 1979.

Schüssler-Fiorenza, Elizabeth, "Feminist Theology as a Critical Theology of Liberation," Theological Studies, 36, no. 4 (December 1975).

Sharpe, Richard, *Medieval Irish Saints' Lives*, Oxford: Clarendon Press, 1991.

Swan, Laura, *The Forgotten Desert Mothers*, Mahwah, NJ: Paulist Press, 2001.

Tavard, George, *Women in Christian Tradition*, South Bend, IN: University of Notre Dame Press, 1973.

Underhill, Evelyn, *Mysticism*, New York: E. P. Dutton, 1961.

Wright, Wendy M., *Bond of Perfection: Jeanne de Chantal and François de Sales*, New York/Mahwah, NJ: Paulist Press, 1985.

Notes

1. Aemiliana Löhr—"The Mother of Salvation," *A Word in Season*, vol. V (Villanova, PA: Augustinian Press, 1995), p. 85.

2. Anahid—*Silent Voices, Sacred Lives* (SVSL), ed. Kathleen Hughes et al. (Mahwah, NJ: Paulist Press, 1992—taken from the book *Holy Women of the Syrian Orient*, translated by Sebastian P. Broch and Susan Ashbrook Harvey, Berkeley: University of California Press, 1987), pp. 147–48.

3. St. Angela Merici—from her *Spiritual Testament*, *A Short Breviary* (Collegeville, MN: St. John's Abbey Press, 1975), pp. 1492–93.

4. *Birgitta of Sweden: The Life and Selected Revelations of Birgitta of Sweden*—CWS #68, (Mahwah, NJ: Paulist Press—from the first revelation in the "Book of Questions" made to Birgitta by the Virgin Mary), p. 105.

5. Ibid., Fifth Book of Revelations, pp. 108–9.

6. Ibid., p. 111.

7. Ibid., p. 118.

8. Ibid., p. 123.

9. Ibid., p. 127.

10. Ibid.

11. Ibid., pp. 135–36.

12. Ibid., p. 145.

13. Ibid., p. 155.

14. Ibid., Seventh Book of Revelations, p. 161.

15. Ibid., p. 167.

16. Ibid., "Four Prayers," p. 223.

17. Ibid., pp. 234–35.

18. Blandina—SVSL, from Eusebius's *Ecclesiastical History* on the martyrs of Lyon and Vienne (AD 177), pp. 96–97.

19. Ibid., p. 114.

20. Brigit of Kildare, *The Wisdom of the Celtic Saints* (WCS) by Edward C. Sellner (Notre Dame, IN: Ave Maria Press, 1993), p. 73.

21. *Catherine of Genoa: Purgation and Purgatory, the Spiritual Dialogue*—CWS #12, 1979, pp. 109–10.

22. *Ibid.*, pp. 144–45.

23. *Ibid.*, pp. 139–40.

24. *Catherine of Siena: The Dialogue*—CWS #17, translated by Suzanne Noffke, OP, 1980, p. 29.

25. Ibid., p. 40.

26. Ibid., p. 41.

27. Ibid., p. 62.

28. Ibid., p. 65.

29. Ibid., p. 72.

30. Ibid., pp. 103–4.

31. Ibid., p. 121.

32. Ibid., p. 126.

33. Ibid., p. 196.

34. Ibid., pp. 278–79.

35. Ibid., p. 357.

36. Dhuoda, *Medieval Women Writers* (MWW), Katharina M. Wilson, ed. (Athens: The University of Georgia Press, 1984), p. 15.

37. Ibid., p. 18.

38. Ibid., p. 20.

39. Ibid., p. 25.

40. Egeria—*The Pilgrimage of Egeria*, taken from *A Lost Tradition: Women Writers of the Early Church* (ALT), ed. Patricia Wilson-Kestner et al. (Lanham, MD: University of America Press, 1981), p. 87 (written from Europe between AD 381 and 388 to her nuns at home).

41. Ibid., p. 119.

42. Ibid., p. 128.

43. Elizabeth—SVSL, *Holy Women of the Syrian Orient*, p. 206.

44. Eudokia—ALT, *Martyrdom of St. Cyprian of Antioch*, pp. 150–51.

45. Ibid., pp. 164–65.

46. Gertrude of Helfta, *The Herald of Divine Love*, CWS #76, Book I (Mahwah, NJ: Paulist Press, 1993), p. 64.

47. Ibid., Book II, p. 97.

48. Ibid., Book II, p. 112.

49. Ibid., Book II, p. 118.

50. Ibid., Book III, p. 184.

51. Ibid., Book III, pp. 188–89.

52. Ibid., Book III, p. 198.

53. *Hadewijch—the Complete Works*, CWS #23, translated by Mother Columba Hart (Mahwah, NJ: Paulist Press, 1980), Letter 2, p. 49.

54. Ibid., Letter 6, pp. 56–57.

55. Ibid., p. 57.

56. Ibid., pp. 58–59.

57. Ibid., p. 61.

58. Ibid., Letter 11, p. 69.

59. Ibid., Letter 24, pp. 103–4.

60. Ibid., poem, "The Paradoxes of Love," p. 344.

61. Hadewijch, SVSL—"Letters," p. 78.

62. Hild of Whitby, WCS, pp. 144–45.

63. Hildegard of Bingen—*Book of Divine Works, with Letters and Songs*, Matthew Fox, ed. (Santa Fe, NM: Bear & Company—now a subsidiary of Inner Traditions International, Rochester, VT—1987), pp. 280–81.

64. Ibid., p. 283.

65. Ibid., p. 292.

66. Ibid., p. 311.

67. Ibid., pp. 334–35.

68. Hildegard of Bingen, MWW, pp. 123–24.

69. Jane de Chantal, *Francis de Sales, Jane de Chantal: Letters of Spiritual Direction*, CWS #59, translated by Peronne Marie Thibert, VHM (Mahwah, NJ: Paulist Press, 1988), to her daughter, the Countess de Toulonjon, p. 218.

70. Ibid., to her brother, the Archbishop of Bourges, pp. 201–2.

71. Ibid., to her brother, the Archbishop of Bourges, pp. 202–3.

72. Ibid., to a religious, Marie-Aimess de Morville, pp. 225–26.

73. Ibid., to Sister Peronne-Marie de Chatel at Lyons, p. 232.

74. Ibid., to Sister Peronne-Marie de Chatel at Lyons, p. 233.

75. Ibid., to Mother Jenne-Charlotte de Brechard, superior at Moulins, pp. 234–36.

76. Ibid., to Mother Peronne-Marie de Chatel, superior at Grenoble, p. 239.

77. Ibid., to the Sisters of the Visitation at Annecy, pp. 239–40.

78. Ibid., to Mother Paule-Jeronyme de Monthoux, superior at Nevers, p. 243.

79. Ibid., to Sister Anne-Marie Rosset, novice mistress at Dijon, pp. 247–48.

80. Ibid., to the superior at Digne, pp. 248–49.

81. Ibid., to Sister Anne-Catherine de Sautereau, novice mistress at Grenoble, pp. 249–50.

82. Ibid., to Mother Marie-Adrienne Fichet, superior at Rumilly, p. 254.

83. Ibid., to a Visitation community, p. 261.

84. Ibid., to a Visitandine, p. 262.

85. Ibid., to a superior, p. 265.

86. Julian of Norwich, *Showings*, CWS #1 Ramsey, NJ: Paulist Press, 1978), pp. 130–31.

87. Ibid., p. 131.

88. Ibid., pp. 164–65.

89. Ibid., p. 197.

90. Ibid., p. 250.

91. Ibid., p. 264 (also in SVSL, pp. 55–56).

92. Ibid., p. 284 (also in SVSL, p. 218).

93. Ibid., p. 285 (also in SVSL, p. 160).

94. Ibid., pp. 296–97 (also in SVSL, p. 55).

95. Ibid., pp. 300–1.

96. Ibid., p. 329.

97. Leoba, *Life of Leoba*, by Rudolf, Monk of Fulda, SVSL, pp. 380–81.

98. Ibid., pp. 381–82.

99. Ibid., pp. 382–83.

100. Ibid., pp. 383–84.

101. Ibid., p. 389.

102. Ibid., p. 390.

103. Margery Kempe—MWW, from *The Book of Margery Kempe*, p. 309.

104. Marguerite Porete—MWW, from *The Mirror of Simple Souls*, pp. 213–14.

105. Martha—SVSL, *Holy Women of the Syrian Orient*, p. 130.

106. *Ibid.*, p. 131.

107. Mechtild of Magdeburg—MWW, from Mechtild of Magdeburg's *The Flowing Light of the Godhead*, p. 168.

108. Ibid., p. 169.

109. Ibid.

110. Ibid., p. 170.

111. Ibid., pp. 171–72.

112. Ibid., pp. 177–78.

113. Ibid., p. 178.

114. Ibid., p. 181.

115. Mechtild of Magdeburg, SVSL, from "True Sorrow," p. 76.

116. Olympias—SVSL, *Life of Olympias*, p. 309.

117. Ibid., p. 312.

118. Ibid., pp. 314–15.

119. Perpetua—ALT, from the *Martyrdom of Perpetua: A Protest Account of Third-Century Christianity*, p. 20.

120. Ibid., pp. 21–22.

121. Ibid., p. 26.

122. Ibid., p. 27.

123. Ibid., p. 28.

124. Ibid., pp. 28–29.

125. Ibid., p. 29.

126. Ibid., p. 29–30.

127. Proba—ALT, from Proba's *Cento*, p. 48.

128. Ibid., pp. 49–50.

129. Ibid., pp. 62–63.

130. Ibid., pp. 66–67.

131. Ruhm, SVSL, from *Holy Women of the Syrian Orient*, p. 95.

132. Sarah—SVSL, from the "Sayings of the Desert Mother Sarah," p. 392.

133. Sibylline Oracles—SVSL, pp. 53–54.

134. Ibid., pp. 283–84.

135. Ibid., p. 284.

136. Syncletica—SVSL, p. 100.

137. Ibid., p. 100–1.

138. Ibid., p. 102.

139. Teresa of Avila, *The Interior Castle*, CWS #14, translated by Kieran Kavanaugh, OCD, and Otilio Rodriguez, OCD (Ramsey, NJ: Paulist Press, 1979)—from "The First Dwelling Places," p. 38.

140. Ibid., p. 43.

141. Teresa of Avila, *The Complete Works of Saint Teresa of Jesus*, translated from the critical edition of P. Silverio De Santa Teresa, CD and edited by E. Allison Peers, Vol. II (Franklin, WI: Sheed & Ward, 1946), p. 406.

142. Ibid., Vol. I ("The Life of the Holy Mother Teresa of Jesus"), p. 65.

143. Ibid., pp. 212–13.

144. Ibid., Vol. II ("Interior Castle"), p. 345.

145. Theodora—SVSL, from the "Sayings of the Desert Mother Theodora," pp. 199–200.

146. Ibid., pp. 200–1.

147. Marie de France, MWW, from the "Fables of Marie de France" (written sometime between 1160 and 1215), pp. 84–85.